Tribe

Tending the Fires
of the Great Spirit Within

First published by O Books, 2010
O Books is an imprint of John Hunt Publishing Ltd., The Bothy, Deershot Lodge, Park Lane, Ropley,
Hants, SO24 0BE, UK
office1@o-books.net
www.o-books.net

Distribution in:

UK and Europe
Orca Book Services
orders@orcabookservices.co.uk
Tel: 01202 665432 Fax: 01202 666219
Int. code (44)

USA and Canada
NBN
custserv@nbnbooks.com
Tel: 1 800 462 6420 Fax: 1 800 338 4550

Australia and New Zealand
Brumby Books
sales@brumbybooks.com.au
Tel: 61 3 9761 5535 Fax: 61 3 9761 7095

Far East (offices in Singapore, Thailand,
Hong Kong, Taiwan)
Pansing Distribution Pte Ltd
kemal@pansing.com
Tel: 65 6319 9939 Fax: 65 6462 5761

South Africa
Stephan Phillips (pty) Ltd
Email: orders@stephanphillips.com
Tel: 27 21 4489839 Telefax: 27 21 4479879

Text copyright Marcus F. Griffin 2009

Design: Stuart Davies

ISBN: 978 1 84694 332 4

A CIP catalogue record for this book is available
from the British Library.

Printed by Digital Book Print

O Books operates a distinctive and ethical publishing philosophy in
all areas of its business, from its global network of authors to
production and worldwide distribution.

Tribe

Tending the Fires
of the Great Spirit Within

Marcus F. Griffin

BOOKS

Winchester, UK
Washington, USA

CONTENTS

CONTENTS

For Heather

Foreword

By Christopher Penczak

The Great Spirit. Of all the names I've learned for 'God' I think I like this one the best. It doesn't denote gender. It doesn't speak of race. It can be applied to so many of our modern mystical paths. Though Native in origin, Great Spirit transcends culture, time or place. The Great Spirit is something we can all relate to regardless of our upbringing, religious training or current belief structure. No matter where we are in our own spiritual journey, we can potentially relate to divinity through the words Great Spirit and understand and empathize with others who also use these words.

The name Great Spirit isn't descriptive of divinity because it is really seeking to describe the Great Mystery, the source of all things that are truly beyond our human understanding. Attempts to name it, shape it and define it precisely lead to the theology of separation and ultimately to our Holy Wars and Inquisitions, just as real today as they were a thousand years ago. In English the word spirit is drawn from the Latin, from 'spiritus', a term for the breath, but also for the invisible life force that supports all things, carried on the breath. It is the animating energy, the subtle life force that all magical cultures have known and is the secret key to the esoteric sciences, including yoga, shamanism and alchemy. So Great Spirit is simply the mysterious source of this life force, this spirit breath. It is the origin of such power. Beyond that, little else can be claimed as definitive. Surrendering to the mystery by using the name Great Spirit allows us each to individually explore it, to seek it out in our own ways, in our own times, building a relationship with divinity that Marcus F Griffin calls 'tending the fires.'

Though the Great Spirit might be unknowable, and the spiritual quest the desire to expand our awareness further until we can know the Great Spirit better, Marcus also provides us with something we can know. He teaches us to find something that is intimately knowable, with its own blessings, challenges and rewards – Tribe. In such Native traditions where the terminology Great Spirit originates, there is another all-important structure to support the spiritual and cultural journey that is Tribe. While being Tribe is knowable, too few of us in the modern world have experienced it. Too few of us have found Tribe. In fact, if you look around, the reciprocal arrangements of community are breaking down. Sure, there are government services for healthcare and welfare in many countries, but they are not the same as tribal community, particularly in America. As our modern sense of community breaks down we have the unique opportunity to build new models, structures and ways of living, and here in your hands is an opportunity to reintroduce the concept of Tribe into your spirituality. Here is a chance to bring the more personal aspects of shamanism to your daily and communal life. Turn the pages and allow Marcus to take you with his teachings, his dreams, visions and insight into a new way of being, or simply remind you of what is already deep within your bones and deep within your soul. Return to tribal consciousness and reframe it for the world yet to come. Blessed be,

Christopher Penczak

Preface

A Shaman by Any Other Name

Greetings reader. Let's look at the plan of this book. You may find it different from books you're used to. In writing this book I discovered that it was a necessity for me to be able to share with you my own personal insights and teachings, plus the stories, dreams and visions that were given to me by what I'll call *the Great Spirit*.

Following this introduction, the teachings in this book are given in sections, each of which contains three or more subsections, or chapters. At the beginning of each section, we will be tagging along on the spiritual journey of *Kasheena the Dreamwalker*, and her quest to become the shaman of her tribe.

In the middle subsections, we will be taking a fair but critical look into the social sciences,[1] religious beliefs, and historical facts and fictions surrounding tribes both ancient and modern. We will then see if we can discover for ourselves the treasures of insight and wisdom waiting to be unearthed. Finally, at the end of each section, we will be doing our own vision questing by following a *Medicine Wheel* [2] that will lead us into the past in search of the Great Spirit within us and within the heart of the great tribe known as humanity, and then back into our ordinary lives today.

Keep in mind, also, that even though I will be showing you the world through the eyes of the shaman and speaking to you by borrowing his voice, this book is not intended to teach you how to become a shaman nor how to practice shamanic medicine. I wrote this book so that we, both you *and* I, could take some time out of our often all-too-hurried 21st-century lives and seek out the light and the sacred spark of the Great

Spirit that dwells within each and every one of us. I wrote this book so that we could gather around the fire and I could share with you some of the stories and traditions that have been passed down to me by my teachers and ancestors. However brief that time may be, we came together for a common reason and a common cause. For one small moment we were as one. We were shamans. We were *tribe*

Prelude to a Dream
The true accounts of March 19, 2005

'Myths and dreams come from the same place. They come from realizations of some kind that find expression in symbolic form'. - Joseph Campbell, *The Power of Myth*

It was eve of the spring equinox, and even though Old Man Winter was still sitting firmly and sourly on his throne in the upper Midwest, our spiritual group had gathered at our home for what would be a pleasant and uplifting night of ceremony, conversation and food. The candles had been lit and the tale of Persephone's ascent had been told most eloquently by one of our members. The time had finally come to relax, and as I sat on a floor carpeted by a bounty of flowers and brightly-colored eggs adorned with supernal symbols, I felt the spirit of the group growing stronger and brighter than it had been in quite some time. Whether it was cold outside or not, in our group spring had come at last. As wine flowed freely from the chalice, the girls began their usual chatter about planting spring flowers, pruning and dressing up the garden for the upcoming warm weather celebrations, while the men did their best to add to the conversation without interrupting. All things considered, I was in pretty good spirits. As the hours of the evening grew late

and my eyes grew weary, however, a problem that had been nagging at me for weeks slowly made its return. It hung over me like a ghost that only I could perceive. I was feeling the unscratchable itch to begin writing another book. It had hit me about a month earlier and even though I knew what I wanted to write about, which was a book that would take the reader (and myself) on a spiritual journey, the right voice with which to write was proving to be as elusive as my new students' quest to find that very same spirit within themselves.

I was watching our group's new members very closely tonight. Not because they needed looking after, but because I knew that they were to be the muses that would guide my words to help them and others like them to find a path to that which they sought. Even though I had my own memories and my own experience with the quest to find the light of the spirit within, the light of those memories had dimmed considerably over the years. Even though I knew that neither I nor any other teacher can simply take a person by the hand and lead them into spirituality, or pull it out of my pocket and present it to them as a gift, I was still their guide and mentor. I knew that I had to do my best to assist them and anyone else I could reach through the written word to find that slippery and elusive divine light know as *spirituality*.

It was getting very late, and as all but a few of our group wished us well and bid us a good night, the busyness of a long day and an even longer night overtook me. The few who still remained seemed wide awake and more than eager to stay up into the wee hours discussing the ceremony, their favorite Anne Rice novels, and all manner of things.

I knew that I wouldn't outlast them and that if I tried to stay awake I would end up falling asleep on the couch and annoying them to distraction with my manly snoring. So I gave my wife and each student a kiss on the top of the head and retreated to the bedroom and the safety and warmth of a down comforter and several overweight cats. As I snuggled into bed and closed my eyes, the events of the evening slowly began playing out in my mind.

The last thing I remembered was a vision of looking down upon all of us who were gathered in a circle like a large and loving family. The vision quickly faded, and just before I slipped into sleep, a single word resounded in my mind ... *tribe*. I began to dream....

Emergence Part One:

Flight of the Dreamwalker

'All that we see or seem is but a dream within a dream.'-
Edgar Allan Poe, *A Dream Within a Dream*

*Our story begins in the dream world, where the dreamer
sleeps, dreams and then awakens into a dream within a
dream...*

*Kasheena awoke in a small wood on the side of a steep hill a few
miles from her village and the lean-to she lived in with her grandmother. This makeshift structure was attached to the side of a small
but inviting mud lodge. You couldn't exactly call it a home, for the
family that had taken them in after her parents died barely had
enough food and shelter for themselves, but they did their best for
their guests. Kasheena's grandmother did the very best she could to
make the lean-to cozy.*

*Kasheena had no idea how long she had been asleep, but by the
blackness of the sky and the brilliance of the stars overhead, she
could tell it must be the middle of the night. Suddenly the
realization of possible failure on her oh-so-important mission hit
her. She quickly rose to her feet and whispered, 'I've got to find him,'
to the darkness. A dragonfly buzzed by her head and disappeared
into the night. An owl in a nearby tree hooted and turned to look at
her. Then it took to the air to continue searching for its supper.
Kasheena watched the huge bird's ascent and for a moment she even
thought about following it to see where it might lead her. All at
once, she spied the silhouette of the shaman high at the top of the
hill.*

*Kasheena had been taught the basics of moving silently through
the woods by one of the hunters in her village, and, although she*

was a far cry from being a master woodsman, she felt confident in her ability to get close to the shaman without his noticing her. She wanted to see what he might be up to. Moving as carefully and quietly as she could, she somehow managed to make it within a few yards of the old wise man without so much as stirring a leaf or breaking a twig. In hope of catching even a small glimpse of the shaman's medicine, she stopped and peered through the blackness of the night.

'You have traveled a long way this night, Dreamwalker,' the shaman said. He hadn't even so much as turned his head, but she instantly knew without question that she had been caught spying on him. Acting as if nothing unusual was happening, Kasheena rose from the undergrowth, brushed the dirt and pine needles from her clothes and said, 'I'm not Dreamwalker, Grandfather. I'm just Kasheena from the village.'

The shaman stood completely still for a moment, waiting to make sure that she had finished speaking. Then he slowly turned to face the brave young girl. His face was old and wrinkled, worn by time and the sun, but pleasing to look upon all the same. The hint of a smile crossed his lips, and the look in his eyes clearly told Kasheena that he was skeptical of what she had said. 'No?' he asked. He shrugged his shoulders and turned away from her once more to look into the valley far below. 'I thought for certain that you were the Dreamwalker,' he continued. 'I thought that you were the one who wanted to learn the ways of medicine and the ways of all tribes. I thought that you were the one who would take my place as shaman after I have gone.'

'Sh-sh-shaman?' she stuttered. "But I thought it was forbidden for a female to become shaman!'

'A true shaman is neither male nor female, neither eagle nor fox, neither human nor spirit.' The old man continued to look off into the dark distance. 'A true shaman,' he said after a moment, 'Is all of these things and none of these things, all at the same time.' He turned to face her. 'Who put the notion into your head that a female could not be a shaman?'

'The boys in the village. They tease me because I told them I wanted to learn about medicine and the Great Spirit.'

The old man nodded. "It's true that the chieftain and many of the village elders are skeptical and resist the idea of a female shaman,' he said, 'but I thought that you might be the one to prove them wrong and change their minds.'

'Me? But I don't know how to be shaman.' She shook her head. 'I could play dress-up and look like a shaman, if I really wanted to, but I don't know how to talk to the spirits and make the medicine.'

'The warriors and hunters of your tribe,' the old man said, 'have learned to approach their quarry not only in the guise of that which they hunt, but also in its mind and spirit. This is what you must find if you are to take my place, little Dreamwalker. You must find the mind and the spirit of the shaman.'

'My tribe?' Kasheena asked, side-stepping entirely the topic of her becoming shaman. 'It's your tribe, too, isn't it?'

'All tribes are one tribe,' the old man replied. 'But very few chieftains, and fewer people, can see and understand this. If they believed that all tribes are one tribe, that all things are one thing, then the Great Spirit would make itself known to them. They would no longer look to the shaman to find it for them.'

The old man smiled down at the girl. His long hide coat was adorned with feathers and beads and had been painted with the symbols of his medicine. In his hand, he carried a long walking-stick fashioned from the branch of an ash tree. It was also adorned with feathers and symbols. 'Will you make the flight this night, Dreamwalker?' he asked. 'Will you fly with the spirits and find your destiny?'

'What! Me? Now?' Kasheena's eyes were as big as full moons. 'But I'm just a little girl. Surely the spirits don't want me!'

The expression on the shaman's face didn't change, and she knew in that instant that he was serious. He wasn't teasing her like the boys in the village always did. Kasheena's face became somber and serious. The shadows of the windswept pines washed over her, making her look much older than she really was. 'If I don't go tonight,' she asked quietly, 'Will I ever get another chance?'

The shaman breathed deeply of the night air and turned his head to gaze down into the valley far below them. 'Impossible to see,' he said without expression. 'The spirit of everything moves in its own time and in its own way. The only thing that I am certain of is that if the Great Spirit did not feel you were ready, it would not have opened the door for you.'

'Door? What door?'

'Can you not see it, Dreamwalker?' The shaman further turned his head to hide the grin that had come over his face. 'Perhaps the spirits don't know as much about you as they think they do.' 'No!' Kasheena almost shouted. 'I mean… could you maybe show me how to see it?

The shaman stood motionless for a moment, and then turned back to the girl and held out his hand. 'Well,' he began, 'I will do the best that an old man can do.'

Feeling about as fearless as a skunk walking into a den of bears, the brave girl stepped forward. 'What do I do?' she whispered.

'Hold my staff in your hand' the old man said, 'And ask the spirits to guide you.'

Kasheena grasped the staff as if she were holding onto it for her very life. Suddenly a strange white light surrounded the staff. Kasheena could feel it gently vibrating in her hands. She could hear a sound like the buzzing of a hive of bees and at that very moment she also noticed that the valley below was beginning to change.

Dots of bright light began appearing everywhere in the valley. Small mounds of earth in the valley's basin turned to gray. They began growing larger and larger, higher and higher. Some of the mounds grew so tall that they almost seemed to disappear into the sky. These huge mounds were also dotted with the strange lights. They seemed to make patterns on the land. Between them, she could see large pathways made of smooth stone.

Without warning, Kasheena's feet left the ground. She began rising into the air and floating over the valley. Strong winds began whipping about her and she could now hear strange sounds echoing everywhere in the valley far below. Her hair thrashing madly around her face in the unearthly winds, she looked back at the shaman. 'Will you come with me?' she shouted to be heard over the high-pitched whistling of the winds.

He shook his head. 'No, little Dreamwalker. Where you are going I cannot follow. But I will be here waiting for you when you return.'

A dragonfly buzzed by Kasheena's head and came to rest on the shaman's shoulder. Kasheena disappeared into the strange village below, a village that had somehow replaced her familiar home.

The Spirit of the Tribe

Tribe. The very word conjures primordial visions and bids us travel beyond the boundaries of what we can see with our eyes. It inspires us to partake of the mystic and the unknown.

The drum sounds and our pulse quickens. Instincts long asleep are stirred ... our bodies and spirits rise to meet its primeval invitation.

Our heart resonates with the sound. Memories long forgotten are renewed. We are drawn to the light of the Great Spirit within.

The drum sounds, and we are called to gather around the fire, to dance and sing and be as one.

Our heart beats in perfect rhythm with the drum. We are called to join together.

We are called to join the tribe.

Tribes are everywhere we look and everywhere we go. They're in our streets, our fields, our jungles, our workplaces and our homes. Tribes are drawn together through common-ality. They're drawn together through common need and mutual interest, for preservation and protection. They're bound to each other by love and blood, by fear and respect. At one time or another, tribes have formed on every continent of our world. They are our clans, our gangs, our clubs and fraternities, our corporations and congresses, our militaries and our families. They are *tribe* ... and each tribe has its own reasons for staying together.

There is a common thread that runs through all tribes, binding them and making them as one: the need to be together. The need to know that we are not alone...

I would hazard to guess that if I were to say the word 'tribe' to a person of Western culture the very first thing they would envision would probably be the Native American peoples of the United States of America. A Westerner of greater imagination might then go on to picture in their mind the Aboriginal tribes of Australia, the Germanic tribes of ancient Europe, or even the often mysterious and secluded tribes of Africa.

I have always felt that the word 'tribe' was more transcendent, that it had a higher, and yet more basic, meaning. To me, the word 'tribe' refers to any group of people who come together for any reason, anywhere, at any time. 'Tribe' can even be used to refer to the individual self, or what I call 'a tribe of one.' Ultimately, to me the word perfectly characterizes the whole of humanity as a single collective: The very spirit of tribalism itself. This is what it means to be *tribe*.

The Great Spirit calls to each and every one of us in a voice we can hear and understand. It reveals itself to us by wearing the face and form we need to see. The Great Spirit embodies the sums of both our needs and our desires. It brings life to our fears and our fantasies, to our disbelief and our recognition of the unknown. The Great Spirit moves through everyone and everything. It is what binds the tribes together. But it is also what separates the tribes and keeps them apart. The Great Spirit is within each and every one of us, waiting in the cracks in our spirits and our minds. It waits in the spaces between what is tangible and real and what is mystic and still unknown. It awaits the moment when we will suspend our disbelief of it and allow it to finally return home; the home inside of us.

We must now set off on a spirit journey to rediscover what it truly means to be *tribe*. We must tend the embers, and re-ignite the fires of the Great Spirit within our hearts and souls. We must retrace the lives and times of the tribes back to their very beginnings. Back to the original sacred spark of the Great Spirit itself.

Please note that throughout this book I will be using the word *tribe* in both its singular and plural forms. Unless otherwise noted, my use of the word should be considered to be a generalization that encompasses the essence or spirit of *all* tribes. It is not meant to single out or delineate any one individual tribe of any ethnicity or members of any ethnic tribe

The Medicine Wheels

You will now begin a quest to reconnect with the spirit of the tribe and rekindle the fires of the Great Spirit within you. Before you can begin your travels, however, you will need a vehicle capable of carrying you to your destination. I have devised a method by which to travel and created a set of visual tools that will help to get you on your way. The method of travel will be a combined form of guided meditation and shamanic ecstasy that I will henceforth refer to as *shamanic traveling*.

We will be taking an in-depth look at this process in the next chapter, but first we need to take a look at the visual tools that will become both the road and the vehicle. These tools will take the form of what are known as *medicine wheels*. While there are many modernized and poeticized definitions of what a medicine wheel is, the anthropological and archeological fact is this: archeologists, anthropologists and scholars have no more than theories, conjectures, and educated guesses as to what medicine wheels were actually used for. While many fascinating theories and possibilities have been suggested, there is no hard evidence to prove any of them. The most widely accepted theory is that medicine wheels held both religious and ritualistic significance to their creators and users.

While researching medicine wheels for this book, I noticed a striking similarity between the way medicine wheels were laid out and artistic renderings of shamanic journeying that I had seen. These artistic similarities included an outer circle, a much smaller inner circle, and lines that seemed to create steps or pathways that led either in or out of the two circles. The circles and pathways closely resemble the wheel, hub and spokes of a medicine wheel. As a result of this revelation, I was able to theorize that medicine wheels might have been used as visual representations of a 'shaman's hole,' which is a hole in the ground, either real or imagined, through which a shaman gains entrance to unseen worlds and hidden realities. This is, of course, pure conjecture on my part, but it's an intriguing possibility nonetheless.

Before we go any further, let's take a moment to look at how medicine wheels were constructed, where the majority of them can be found, and how and where the term *medicine wheel* [3] was first applied.

Scattered across North America are thousands upon thousands of stone structures, the majority of which are simple cobblestone circles associated with the Plains Indians. These are commonly known as "tipi rings." There are also many extremely large stone circles, some measuring upwards of 90 feet in diameter, which invoke a somewhat more esoteric sensation in those who have seen them in person. The most famous and intriguing of these circles are known as "medicine wheels."

The term *medicine wheel* was first given to the Big Horn Medicine Wheel[4] in northern Wyoming, which is also the southernmost medicine wheel still known to exist in modern times. The word 'wheel' was applied to these structures because, basically, that's what many of them look like: huge stone wagon wheels laid on the ground, with an outer circle of stones, a central inner hub and, in some cases, cobblestone lines or spokes radiating from the central hub to the edge of the outer circle. The 'medicine' part of the name implies that these stone structures held religious and/or ceremonial significance to their creators, the native peoples of North America.

Archeologist John Brumley, from Medicine Hat, Alberta, Canada was the first to state that a stone structure must have at least two of the following three traits to be considered a true medicine wheel:

1. A central stone cairn, or hub
2.. One or more concentric stone circles
3. Two or more stone lines radiating from a central point.[5]

While nearly every medicine wheel has its own distinct appearance and form, medicine wheels have been classified into eight different categories or types based upon their general shape. In your shamanic travels, you will be using three of the eight types of medicine wheels. Below are diagrams of these three types of medicine wheels.

The first medicine wheel you will be using (see diagram 1) is classified by Brumley as a 'type 2 medicine wheel.' It repre-

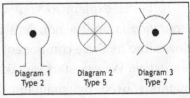

Diagram 1
Type 2

Diagram 2
Type 5

Diagram 3
Type 7

sents the beginning of your journey, the 'door' you will use to gain access to the inner, type 5, medicine wheel (see diagram

2). You can see that the type 2 medicine wheel clearly contains a passageway that leads in or out of the circle. This provides you with the perfect entrance or exit to begin and end each part of your journey. This first medicine wheel is thus the staging point for your shamanic travels.

The second medicine wheel, also known as a type 5 medicine wheel (see diagram 2), represents the path or paths that you will be using to travel deep into your spiritual self. It is also the road that will lead you back through the ages in hopes of discovering the very beginnings of human spirituality. It will also be the road that will lead you back to your present world and identity.

The third medicine wheel, also known as a type 7 medicine wheel (see diagram 3), represents the outer path, the 'spiritual radiance' that will emanate from you after you have discovered or rediscovered the true light and meaning of the Great Spirit within you.

To summarize, the first medicine wheel represents the gateway, the second, the inward journey, and the third, the outward journey. If this seems a bit confusing right now, don't fret. Each step will be clearly described as we go along. Now that you have the 'why' and the 'way' of shamanic traveling, the time has come to take a closer look at the 'how.'

Shamanic Traveling Through Meditation

Emergence. n. A recovering of consciousness - Merriam-Webster Medical Dictionary

To better explain to you what *shamanic traveling* through *meditation* is and is not, let's begin by breaking this phrase down into its three component words: *shamanic, traveling,* and *meditation*. We can start by taking a look at a few of the basic methods used by shamanic practitioners to journey into altered states of consciousness and gain access to different levels of hidden reality. Let's see how these shamanic techniques differ from meditative techniques. This altered state, which is commonly referred to as 'ecstasy,' is described by Hillary S Webb in her book *Exploring Shamanism* as being: '...a process in which, through any one of a number of intentional means, the shaman separates his or her soul from the body, releasing it to travel into one or more of the three spirit worlds. [6] For your spiritual journey, you will be combining the techniques of achieving shamanic ecstasy and guided meditation together. You will thus be taking your first steps onto the path of shamanic traveling.

When I first began doing my own shamanic journeying, I noticed that many of the initial techniques suggested in the books I had read by master shamans to attain a state of ecstasy were very similar to the techniques used to attain a state of deep meditation. There were, however, a few minor, although significant, differences. For example, it is suggested by many modern shamanic practitioners that shamanic journeying is best attempted while in a very comfortable relaxed state and with as little distraction as possible, as is often recommended for attaining a state of deep meditation. Unlike meditation, however, it is also suggested by many of today's leading experts in the field of shamanism that shamanic journeying should always be done in a pitch-black room if possible (or that the shamanic traveler should cover his or her eyes to block out all sources of light), that he or she should be lying on the floor (instead of sitting upright as I would personally recommend for meditation) and that primal, rhythmic drumming (or another suitable form of music, such as anything relaxing and non-verbal, as suggested by Webb) should be played in the shamanic traveler's presence.

Also, unlike meditation, the shamanic traveler uses an established 'door' to begin his or her journey into ecstasy. This door is usually some type of opening that leads down into the ground, like a cave, an animal burrow, a hollow tree stump, a natural spring, etc. that the shaman envisions their spirit entering into to begin their journey into ecstasy. While I have known people who have used a similar induction to begin their meditations, most people who have mastered meditative techniques do not usually start out on a preconceived path. They leave themselves open to any and all possibilities, and allow their subconscious and their imagination to guide them.

The main goal of attaining a state of shamanic ecstasy is to transcend the normal state of consciousness and enter into the spirit worlds to gain power and knowledge, not to center on the core of one's being, as is often the goal of meditation. In other words, although through meditation we can travel to pretty much anywhere we can imagine and play out virtually any scenario in our mind, the main purpose of meditation is usually to discover how and why we fit into these scenarios so we can become better attuned to them and to ourselves. We can also learn from our meditation as we gain a better understanding of the role we play in the web of life.

What you will be attempting to do through shamanic traveling is to enter into a state of shamanic ecstasy, but with very specific directions and goals in mind. The path you seek is the one that will lead you back to the very origin of human spirituality itself. Exactly what this spiritual origin is and what path you will be traveling to find it will be explained in great detail in a later chapter of this book. You will walk along this path one step at a time, and as you reach the goal of each step (journey), your attainment of that goal will lead you deeper and deeper into the medicine wheel, thus ever closer to the fires of the Great Spirit within and the spirit of the tribe itself. The process for attaining a state of shamanic ecstasy will be the same for each of your journeys, but the goal(s) and direction of each journey will be laid out for you ahead of time. You'll have a spiritual roadmap. I'll explain this process in great detail and lay out the step-by-step process for you in *Shamanic Traveling, Path One: Emergence*. That's where you will begin the first leg of your spiritual journey.

As you implement the techniques of shamanic traveling that I will lay out for you, you'll reach the paramount outcome when you learn how to open up the central core of your being to the light and power of the Great Spirit within you, to allow its sacred flame to impassion and motivate you, to allow yourself to become the enlightened spiritual being that you were always meant to be.

To do so, you will now take on the essence of the shaman and allow me to guide your first few steps onto the path of shamanic traveling, the first steps that will eventually lead you back through the ages to reclaim the sacred and vital spark of human spirituality.

Tending the Fires Goal One:
Acquiring the Outer Wheel

The two main goals for your first exercise in shamanic traveling will be to begin connecting with the spirit of the tribe and to acquire (by way of guided shamanic ecstasy) the outer (type 2) medicine wheel (see page 15) which will serve as the entrance or 'gateway' to the inner medicine wheel and its many possible paths that you will eventually be choosing from.

You will need to do a bit of preparation before you can begin this first leg of your spiritual journey. You have a few choices to make. Before we begin, therefore, we should take a look at the mental and/or physical tools you will be using to help you attain a state of shamanic ecstasy and to achieve the goals in each of your journeys. Keep in mind that the tools you decide to use for your first journey will be used for all of your future journeys and for the sake of consistency and stability should not be changed once they have been established. All of the *physical* tools are optional. Keep this in mind as we look at each of them and the purpose they serve.

The first tool is the *shaman's drum*. The importance of shamanic drumming to achieve a state of ecstasy was emphasized in nearly every book I read on shamanism. The shaman's drum is rich in symbolism and cosmic significance. By far, the most captivating description and in-depth explanation of the shaman's drum, as well as its symbolisms and meaning, can be found in chapter 5 of *Shamanism, Archaic Techniques of Ecstasy* by Mircea Eliade. If you would like to do further study into the significance of the shamans drum (or shamanism in general), I highly recommend this book. For the purpose of shamanic traveling, however, consider the following quotation from chapter 5:

> The shamanic drum is distinguished from all other instruments of the 'magic of noise' precisely by the fact that it makes possible an ecstatic experience. Whether this experience was prepared, in the beginning, by the charm of the sounds of the drum, a charm that was evaluated as 'voice of the spirits,' or an ecstatic experience was attained through the extreme concentration provoked by a long period of drumming, is a problem that does not concern us at present. But one fact is certain: it was musical magic that determined the shamanic function of the drum, and not the antidemonic magic of noise.[7]

I myself have always felt that there was a great magical power in music, especially in the primordial sound of the drum and its possible relationship to the beating of a human heart. Intrigued by what my trusty dictionary of symbols might have to say about the drum, I pulled the book from its resting place on the shelf. What I read brought a smile to my face: 'Of all musical instruments, the drum is the most primeval means of communication, its percussive sound traveling to the heart, and, by extension, suggesting the ability to communicate with supernatural forces.[8]

I was pleased that I'd taken the extra time to re-read chapter 5 in Eliade and looked up the symbolism of the drum. Both sources reinforced how I plan to teach you to use drumming to initiate shamanic traveling. It is necessary to have the sound of the drum work its magic by not only speaking to the heart of the shamanic traveler, but also connecting with the 'heart' of the tribe, and thus communicating with the Great Spirit itself.

This is the significance of the shaman's drum. Drumming is also, if you decide to incorporate it, one of the first steps you will use to begin your shamanic traveling to attain a state of ecstasy. If you don't currently own a drum, or don't feel you are competent enough to play one (and don't worry, if *I* can drum, *anybody* can), then you are certainly not required to go out and buy one. It is through the rhythmic beating of the drum that you will be connecting to your heart and the heart of the tribe, so there is no reason why you couldn't go directly to the source and focus in on your own heartbeat to achieve the same effect. This approach, however, is much more complicated and may take a bit more time and practice on your part, depending on your past occult experiences and current level of magical prowess. I wouldn't recommend taking this approach unless you are adept at magical practice and meditative technique, so consider both of these options carefully and make the decision that's right for you before you begin your shamanic traveling.

The second tool you will be using on your journey is a single source of light, such as a candle, a small lantern, or even an imagined (although visualized) light of 'spiritual luminescence,' which you will use to focus in on the Great Spirit within you. Before we continue with the subject of light, let me caution you about fire. If you decide to use an open flame as a tool during your shamanic travels, please understand that the entranced state of shamanic ecstasy can be a transcendent experience, but while in this altered state you can also easily lose track of time and your earthly reality. Be sure to take every precaution to make sure that the flame isn't too close to you or anything flammable. You don't want to set the house on fire while you're 'away' from the mundane world. Make sure that the candle is in a suitable fireproof container. Make sure the lantern is in a safe place. Again, make your choice about using a flame wisely and consider what is best for you. Although symbols can be very powerful mental and visual tools, a living flame is not always just a symbol.

Also remember that the true light resides in you and not the candle's flame. The light of the Great Spirit is always around us. There is no need to go in search of it. The spiritual light that shines within each of us is often harder to see and believe in. Seek out the light inside you and tend the fires of the Great Spirit within.

Once you have weighed your options and made your decisions, gather your drum and your flame, be they physical or magical, real or imagined. Let me lead you along the path of your first expedition in shamanic traveling. ⸱

Shamanic Traveling Path One:
The Spirit Lands

The goal of your first journey is to locate and claim the outer medicine wheel. This first wheel will serve as an entrance into the second or 'inner' medicine wheel, which you will claim on a future journey. It is also the staging point from which you will begin all of your future shamanic travels. As you recall, the outer (type 2) medicine wheel has an obvious opening, or 'gateway,' as well as a short corridor that leads into the wheel's inner circle. (If you don't remember this, refer to the drawing of the type 2 medicine wheel on page 15. You will not be concerning yourself with entering the wheel's gateway for now, only with locating it. To do this, you will be entering into an altered state of consciousness, which will be very similar to attaining a state of shamanic ecstasy, with the only real differences being that you will enter into this state with very specific directions and goals in mind.

We will refer to the specific place you will be attempting to travel to on your first journey as your 'spirit land.' The spirit land will represent an area of claimed spiritual space on which you will find the first medicine wheel. Your spirit land will not exist on either the mundane plane or in the spirit worlds, but somewhere between them. Precisely where your spirit land is located and what it looks, feels and sounds like is up to you and you alone to discover. I cannot guide your footsteps once you have entered into your ecstatic state. I can only tell you what to look for. You have to locate the spirit land and the first medicine wheel for yourself.

This may sound like a pretty tall order if you're not adept at shamanic practice, meditation or astral travel, but I can assure you that if you desire it enough, try long and hard enough and ask the spirits to guide you, you will most certainly be able to locate your spirit land and the medicine wheel. You can reach the goals of your first journey. If for some reason you are unsuccessful in attaining an ecstatic state or meeting the goal of this journey on your first few attempts, *don't give up*. We all have different levels of natural talent, experience and ability. Learning to achieve a state of shamanic ecstasy and mastering meditative techniques is just like learning to do anything else. The more you practice doing it, the more proficient you will become at it. *No one* becomes the master of anything overnight!

To begin your first journey, you will need to prepare a room in your home to be suitable for shamanic traveling. This room should be as dark as possible and as far away as possible from any other activity (noise, family, etc.). You don't want to be distracted during your journey. For obvious reasons, therefore, shamanic traveling is best done at night. I had limited success with shamanic traveling in the outdoors, so unless you live in a very secluded area and are experienced at the art of 'tuning in' and then 'tuning out' the natural world around you, shamanic traveling is also best attempted indoors.

Next, you want to make sure you have stocked your shamanic room with everything you need (drum, candle, lighter or matches, liquid refreshment, etc.) before you darken the room and begin your journey. Also, make sure that you've done everything that you need to do to make yourself as physically comfortable as possible beforehand. Attempting shamanic traveling if you are overly tired, hungry, stuffed with food, ill, or have to go to the bathroom is not a good idea. Make yourself as physically comfortable as possible before you begin.

Note: Whether you have decided to use a drum or your own heartbeat, a candle or a visualized light, for the sake of ease of description I will use the words 'drum' and 'candle.'

Now, to begin the process of shamanic traveling, follow these steps:

1. Darken the room, loosen your clothing (or remove it entirely if you prefer), and remove your shoes and socks.

2. Before you light your candle, become comfortable with the darkness and spend a few moments clearing your mind of mundane thoughts.

3. Without overly focusing on your goal and the impending journey, meditate on what the Great Spirit means to you and how you hope to enrich your mundane and spiritual lives by moving closer to its sacred flame.

4. When you're ready, light your candle. Imagine other small lights that might be out there illuminating the darkness of the world. One by one, try to see as many of these lights as you can in your mind.

5. Imagine the *spiritual light* that exists within you, and within each and every member of the collective tribes. See all of these spiritual lights joining together and building into a great fire of sacred light.

6. Once you are able to see this great fire and can feel its flame warming you, pick up your drum, gaze into the flame of the candle and softly and slowly pound a heartbeat rhythm. With each beat of the drum, feel the sound resonate within you. Feel it connecting with your own heartbeat.

7. Always keeping your vision focused on the flame of the candle, begin to beat the drum a bit faster, a bit louder. With each beat of the drum, feel the heartbeat of another tribal member joining in and connecting with your own.

8. Build this vision, this feeling. Feel the sacred fire growing all around you. Increase the speed and volume of the heartbeat you are pounding out on the drum.

9. Build the number of heartbeats and feel them connecting with your own until the sound of beating hearts, the heat of the sacred fire and the sensation of being surrounded by the tribe fills your spirit and your mind. Build it until you can feel the spirit of the tribe within you and all around you. Build it until you have become one with it.

10. Stop beating the drum and close your eyes.

What you will see when you close your eyes is impossible for me to predict, but through your connection with the tribal spirit, a pathway of some sort should open up before you. You might even see a spirit guide waiting at the beginning of the pathway to assist you. If you don't see this pathway right away, don't give up. Let your mind and spirit drift until it appears. Once it has opened up before you, follow it until it leads you into your spirit land.

Explore this new land until you have located the first medicine wheel. Once you have located the first wheel, investigate it thoroughly until you are acquainted with how it looks and feels. *Under no circumstances*, however, should you enter into the corridor of the wheel at this time. You will enter into the circle of the first wheel in your second journey. I have a very specific destination planned for you to reach at the end of your final exercise in shamanic traveling and entering into the wheel prematurely could greatly compromise my ability to guide you to this location.

After you have investigated your spirit land and found the first medicine wheel, return to the pathway and follow it until you can see a dim light ahead. This light is the flame of the

27

candle burning in your room in the mundane world. Follow the pathway to the light until it becomes so bright that it is all that you can see in your mind's eye.

Open your physical eyes and allow your mind and spirit to return to the earthly plane.

It is possible that on your first journey you will be able to see and experience many things in addition to the pathway, the spirit land and the medicine wheel. Your land may be populated with any combination of tribes, spirits, shamans, animals, or anything else you might imagine. Each experience will be unique to each shamanic traveler. Before turning on the lights, extinguishing the candle and packing up your drum, therefore, spend some time reflecting on your first journey. Many things may be revealed to you during this time of reflection that may not have seemed significant or relevant to you during the journey itself. I am also going to suggest that you take the time to journal your experiences and revelations so that you will have a clear and concise record of your shamanic travels for future reference and study.

You have now tended the embers and moved one step closer to the sacred spark of the Great Spirit and the living heart of the tribe. With each journey you will move closer to the light of your own spirituality. With each journey you will build the fire of the Great Spirit within.

Sacred Symbols

Many of the world's tribes, both ancient and modern, have developed or adopted unique symbols, emblems, or markings that distinguish them from all other tribes. We can look at a tribe's symbol as its visual ambassador, a representative that shows other tribes who and what 'my tribe is' and 'what the tribe stands for.' In our larger towns and metropolitan areas, the use of tribal symbols is so widespread that the symbols litter the urban landscape.

Almost everywhere we look - in our streets, our schools, our factories, our shopping centers, yes, even in our own homes and on the clothes we wear and the gear we carry - we are surrounded by tribal symbols: Corporate logos and trademarks, brand names and badges. We are constantly being greeted by family crests, signet rings, school uniforms and the totem animals of sports teams, which have been imprinted on just about anything you can think of. Our subway cars, buses and trains, our alleys and walls, even our underground caverns have been marked by the aerosol signatures of street gangs and taggers. Even our governmental officials, who in many ways can be considered our elected chieftains, have over time developed a set of symbols that they use to control how we interact with society and how we respond in public. Traffic signs have symbols (the familiar octagon 'stop,' the triangular warning sign, etc.) that tell us when to stop, when to go, in which direction we can go and how fast we are allowed to go there. Other signs tell us where we can stand or not stand (X, which means "Don't do this") where to sit or not sit, and how long we can stand or sit there. Other signs show us where we may smoke, drink, eat, swim, or fish, and where we can and cannot ride our bicycles.

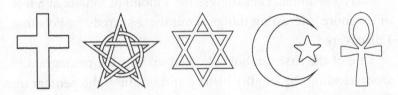

In most cases, these tribal symbols are meant to serve only to protect us from ourselves, but our tribes and their individual members also use very powerful *sacred* symbols as well. And these sacred symbols have inspired many a conflict between the tribes.

The crucifix, the cross, the pentagram, the Star of David,

the Moslem crescent, the ankh and countless other sacred symbols have been used by the tribes for millennia to denote that which (to them) is divine and holy. Many tribes view (or have viewed) their sacred symbols as being so powerful that if they are scoffed at or trifled with, it is an insult of unequaled magnitude. Because of the intolerance of some tribes for the sacred symbols of other tribes, wars have been waged, people have been murdered and entire tribes have been wiped from the face of the earth. Sometimes, just the mere sight of another tribe's sacred symbol has been enough to send other tribes into frenzy. Sacred symbols have usurped the spirit and meaning of the Great Spirit itself, and the true meaning behind sacred symbols has often been lost.

Intrigued by the possibility that some, if not all, of the sacred symbols used by the tribes of the earth possibly held deeper meanings, and perhaps even different origins, than are commonly known by most people (including myself), I headed for the bookstore in search of a good book on the subject of symbols. Not only did I find what I think is one of the best books available on the subject *The Complete Dictionary of Symbols* by Jack Tresidder, [9] but after a long night of reading, I also learned many fascinating things about sacred symbols. Let's digress for a moment to look at a few of the more interesting things about these sacred symbols that I discovered.

One of the first symbols I looked up was the pentagram.[10] Upon reading the lengthy history and origin of the pentagram presented in the book, I must admit that I felt embarrassed that I didn't know more about the history of my personal sacred symbol. Much of what I read was not new, but I was nevertheless surprised by just how much of this symbol's meaning I had taken at face value from the very beginning of my spiritual studies. For example, I had no idea that at one time Christians associated the pentagram with the five wounds of Christ, or that to Pythagoreans, the pentagram represented the numeral 2 (terrestrial and feminine) combined with the number 3, (heavenly and masculine) resulting in the number 5, which symbolizes the microcosm of the human body and mind. Imagine how embarrassed I felt, after *decades* of magical practice and study (the whole time wearing a pentagram as a symbol of my magic), when I learned that the pentagram originated in Mesopotamia around 4000 years ago and that its shape was most likely an astronomical plotting of the movement of the planet Venus through the sky.

This revelation really got the wheels in my head turning and I started wondering just how many other sacred religious symbols being used by the various tribes on the planet had origins and meanings that might be unknown to some, if not most, of their peoples. I thumbed back through the book to find the symbols that began with the letter C. There I found what I was looking for, 'cross.' My suspicions about the origins of this sacred symbol, which of course was adopted by Christianity after the prophet Jesus was crucified on one, were about to be verified.

I discovered that the cross, one of today's most widely used and universally recognizable sacred tribal symbols, had much more ancient meanings and origin than I am willing to bet most of its modern wearers are aware of.

The cross is probably the most transcendent of all the sacred symbols, appearing in one form or another throughout recorded history on almost every continent and spanning across a large number of differing cultures, tribes and religions. In its myriad forms, the cross has ancient roots, uses and origins, some possibly predating its Christian adoption by millennia. The cross has been used to symbolize the cosmos in its simplest form. It has been used to symbolize the four cardinal directions and the four rain-bearing winds. It has been the symbol of fertility, life, kindling energy and even the four great gods of the elements. It has been the Chinese symbol of earth and stability, the Hindu emblem representing the fire sticks of Agni, [11] and the Buddhist wheel of life. As the swastika, it has been used as an emblem of cosmic energy and it was also a summary of the Tree of Life. With the addition of a circle, it became the Celtic cross, which probably represented a blending of pagan and Christian symbolism. In Egypt, it took on the form of the ankh, also known as 'the key of life,' symbolizing immortality. And of course, the cross became an integral part of the symbol of the crucifixion of the Christian savior.

So many symbols, so many meanings, so much blending and intertwining of religious beliefs, so many common roots. And yet, to this day, so little tolerance and understanding among the tribes.

It is not enough to understand the problems that have been associated with tribes because of their religious beliefs and sacred symbols. It is not enough to accept prejudice and hatred generated by the religious intolerance as things we cannot change. If we were to walk a mile in the moccasins of a member of another tribe, we might see that not only have the sacred symbols of the tribes and the religious beliefs for which they stand co-existed peacefully side by side for centuries, but also that they can continue to co-exist peacefully into the future.

Emergence Part Two:
The Sacrifice

Kasheena awoke on the bank of a wide, slow-moving stream. She looked around sleepily and immediately noticed that something was moving towards her through the tall grass. Curious but uncertain, she rose quickly to her feet and took a few cautious steps backwards. All at once, a large turtle poked its head through the grass and looked up at her shyly. The sight of the creature was enough to bring a smile to her face, and she watched with some small amusement as the turtle turned away from her and slowly struggled its way out of the tall grass, seemingly eager to reach the safety and ease of movement the water had to offer. The turtle entered the stream, swam into an eddy that whirled along the bank, and finally came to rest near a large pile of stones on the eddy's sandy bottom.

Moving closer to the edge of the stream so she could get a closer look at the turtle, Kasheena caught her own reflection on the surface of the water, which glistened and twinkled under the filtered sunlight shining through the lazily swaying treetops high above. Kasheena was transfixed by the beauty of the dancing water-lights and the life that flourished near the stream. She gazed with satisfaction at her reflection on the water and, just for a moment, her reflection seemed to change, making her look much older than she really was. She began to question this strange vision, when suddenly the flash of something sparkling in the pile of rocks at the bottom of the eddy caught her eye. Before she even realized what she was doing, Kasheena had slid into the water herself and was wading through the eddy's shallow wash toward the pile of stones.

She kept a close eye on the turtle, which was still resting on the sandy bottom near the pile of stones. The girl moved as slowly as she could, being careful not to splash or make any sudden movements, for she didn't want to scare the poor thing off. As she neared the pile of stones, she saw the flash of mystical light again. Without hesitation, she reached deep into the water, soaking her hair and clothing. She seized the sparkling object from the pile of stones at her feet. What could this sparkling object be? Opening her hand and looking more closely at what she had picked up, she felt more confusion than excitement. Instead of the magical treasure she had expected, she was holding only a simple smooth, black stone with no distinguishing features of any kind. She rolled the stone in her hand, trying to get it to sparkle in the sunlight. No sparkle. Thinking that she might have picked up the wrong stone, she peered into the waters again. Maybe she would see another flash of light.

'Wow!' An enthusiastic voice suddenly sounded from somewhere behind her. 'That's a healing stone! Those are a rare find these days.'

Startled, Kasheena turned too quickly and lost her footing in the soft sand. Righting herself, she made a whole circle. Who had spoken to her? She saw no one. Had she imagined the voice? All at once, she noticed that the turtle had surfaced and was now floating a few feet away from her. It seemed to be looking her in the eye.

'What are you staring at, you stupid turtle?' she snapped, suddenly feeling lost and alone.

'Unless you have an invisible playmate standing next to you,' the turtle responded, 'I must be looking at you.'

Kasheena stared at the turtle. Certain that she was imagining things, she said aloud, 'Turtles can't talk!'

'And little girls can't be shamans,' the turtle replied in a matter-of-fact voice. 'So that leaves both of us in a rather awkward predicament, don't you think?' Without waiting for her to reply, the turtle added, "By the way, I'm not really supposed to be here, so keep your voice down a little if you please.'

'What do mean, you're not supposed to be here?' She couldn't help but think how silly she felt speaking to an imaginary talking turtle. But she was a curious girl. 'Where are you from?' she asked it.

'Well, that's kind of difficult to explain,' the turtle replied. It

seemed uncertain about whether or not it wanted to answer the question. It turned its gaze away from her as it considered its choice, then looked her in the eye again. 'Okay,' it said. 'You're supposed to be figuring this stuff out for yourself, but I don't suppose it would hurt if I gave you a little help. I'm from what is known as the lower world. I'm your animal spirit. I'm here to help you with your quest to become shaman.'

'Really? You're my animal spirit?'

'None other.'

'What kinds of things are you going to teach me?' The girl was barely able to contain her excitement. 'Then what are we waiting for? Let's get started!'

'Whoa!' the turtle cried out. 'You'd better put a leash on that enthusiasm before it gets you into trouble. The first thing I'm going to teach you is that faster isn't always better. You need to slow down and think things out before you act. Have you taken a good look at your surroundings yet? Do you even know where you are?'

'No.' Kasheena looked down at her feet through the sunlit water. 'I haven't looked around. I don't know where I am or even how I got here. This is all so strange,' she continued with a sigh. 'It all seems like a dream.'

"Technically,' the turtle said, 'this is a dream and you're smack-dab in the middle of it. But this place is also what the shamans call the middle world. The middle world is filled up with people, animals, plants... that kind of stuff. You know - nature.'

'You mean I'm dreaming all of this?' Kasheena asked, a skeptical look coming into her eyes.

'I didn't say you were dreaming,' the turtle responded. 'I said you are in a dream.'

Suddenly a third voice joined what both girl and turtle thought was a private conversation. 'Is this yours?'

'His dream, to be precise,' the turtle said with a chuckle.

Kasheena turned toward the sound of the voice and again lost her footing in the soft sand of the bottom of the stream. This time she *came crashing down in a large splash.*

As she pushed herself up, her ears were filled with the familiar sound of boyish laughter. The shock from her wet fall was instantly replaced by the shame of being laughed at, then by anger. These were feelings she knew all too well.

A giggling boy was standing on the bank above her. What Kasheena saw in his hand inflated her anger to the point of near rage. The boy was holding the shaman's staff.

Kasheena scrambled to her feet and emerged from the water looking more like a wild animal than a little girl. Rage shone in her squinted eyes and clenched teeth. She was even growling. Without warning, she charged the boy and struck him in the chest with her shoulder, knocking him to the ground. 'What's the matter with you?' she shouted as she bent over the fallen boy and wrenched the shaman's staff from his hand. 'You don't steal from people and you don't laugh at them,' she scolded. 'You're just like the boys in my village. I wish you were dead!'

She took several steps backwards, raising the shaman's staff above her head. All at once the realization of what she had just said took hold. Her anger was replaced by shame. Again, she had acted without thinking. She would have to do her best to make amends.

She lowered the staff and tried to smile, then took a small step forward. She looked down at the boy. 'Are-are you OK?' There was no response. 'I ... I didn't mean to hurt you... I....' She paused mid-sentence. The boy was crying. That was unexpected. 'What have I done?' she whispered, more to herself than to the boy.

The boy looked up through tear-filled eyes. 'You'll get your wish soon enough, you hateful girl.' He slowly pulled himself into a sitting position. 'This was the only safe place I had left, you know,' he continued. 'Now I can't even dream without being reminded that I'm going to die."'

'What do you mean, you're going to die?' Bending down, Kasheena took him gently by the arm and helped him to stand.

'I'm sick,' he replied, 'and the doctors don't know what's wrong

36

with me.' He was obviously comforted by her concern and soft touch. 'My parents don't think I know,' he continued, 'but I do. I overheard the doctors telling them I don't have very much time left.'

'Doctors? What's a doctors?'

'Not a doctors, you silly girl,' the boy replied, a wide grin coming over his face. 'Just doctor. You know, the person that gives you medicine and tries to make you feel better.'

Kasheena nodded. 'Medicine,' she said. 'I know about medicine.' She led the boy into a shadier spot under a nearby tree and helped him sit on a big, moss-covered root. 'Is doctor the name of your tribe's shaman?' she asked him.

'Tribe? Shaman? What in the world are you talking about?' The boy looked up at her. 'I don't know what a shaman is. I don't belong to a tribe. I belong to a family.'

"How can you not know what a shaman is?" Kasheena looked at him as if he were joking. 'Are you teasing me? And what do you mean, you don't belong to a tribe? Are you and your family outcasts?'

'Outcasts?' The boy looked totally bewildered. 'Well,' he said, 'We don't have much money, but we sure aren't outcasts. We live in a small house near the edge of town.'

'Money? Town?' Kasheena was starting to wonder who this foreigner was and if he knew anything at all. 'I don't know what village you're from,' she said, 'But it sure sounds like a strange place., She sat down beside him, though not too close. 'Forgive my discourtesy. I haven't introduced myself. My name is Kasheena.'

The boy raised an eyebrow. 'That's a weird name.'

Kasheena's eyes narrowed, but this time she was able to keep her temper under control.

'Well,'' the boy said, also suddenly remembering his manners, 'I'm pleased to meet you, Kasheena. My name's Daniel.'

'Daniel.' Kasheena almost giggled. 'And you think I have a weird name?'

And these two children, born in different times and cultures, both started giggling, and once started, they couldn't stop themselves. Within minutes, they were up and dancing out of the shade, still giggling and poking fun at each othe, and at last they fell down on the warm, sunlit grass by the stream, still giggling. After a while however, Kasheena's laughter faded and a concerned expression came over her face.

'My animal spirit told me that all of this is just a dream,' she said solemnly. 'It told me that this is your dream and I'm just in it. Is that true?'

'Yeah, that's true.' Daniel looked at the stream and the trees, then back at the girl. 'But what I don't understand,' he said in a puzzled voice, 'Is what you're doing in it. We've never met before, have we?'

'No,' Kasheena said, 'We've never met before, and, to tell the truth, I'm not even sure how I got here.'

And at that very moment, a word the shaman had used, an epithet he had used to address her at the top of the hill surfaced in the girl's memory. Dreamwalker. In some way she still didn't understand, Kasheena's strange journey was starting to make sense.

'There's something I have to do here,' she whispered, more to herself than to Daniel, 'Something to do.'

'What could you possibly have to do in my dream?' Suddenly there was condescension in the boy's voice.

'I'm not sure,' she said, 'But maybe my animal spirit knows.'

Daniel shook his head in confusion. 'What the heck is an animal spirit?'

'Why, there's an animal spirit.' She pointed at the stream, where the turtle was swimming but - no, the turtle was gone. She had been about to explain to Daniel what an animal spirit was, but now she jumped up and ran to the water. The turtle was nowhere to be seen. 'Oh, no,' she cried. 'Where are you?' She looked upstream and downstream. No turtle. 'Please come back, she begged. 'I'll be good this time.' she promised.

She was just about to jump back into the stream to search for the turtle, when she spied it resting under a nearby tree. 'Oh, There you are. I thought you'd left...me...' She stopped. All that remained of the turtle was an empty shell. 'What have I done?' She fell to her knees next to the shell. Certain that her actions had caused the turtle to disappear, the girl picked up the empty shell, and with hope beyond hope wished for the turtle to return. It did not.

At that very moment, however, Kasheena noticed something quite interesting. The healing stone she had pulled from the bottom of the stream, the stone forgotten during her conversation with Daniel, was now lying on the ground close to where she had found the shell, and the glyph of a turtle was now somehow carved into its smooth-black surface.

Unable to resist, Kasheena picked up the healing stone and gripped it tightly in her hand. The dreamworld around her began to change. A vision of the lower world opened up before her, and through the otherworldly haze of the vision she began to see the turtle slowly moving towards her, its form ghostlike.

'Daniel is dying, little Dreamwalker.' The turtle's words became clearer as the spirit came nearer to her.

Kasheena had no idea if she was hearing the turtle's voice with her ears or in her mind, but she listened intently just the same.

'No earthly medicine can cure the boy,' the spirit turtle continued. 'It is his spirit and his will to live alone that can save him. You must heal Daniel's spirit and give him the courage to fight his illness. If you do not, his earthly life will be lost.'

'But...but I don't know how. I don't know what to do.'

'Hah,' the turtle scoffed. 'Are you not the bravest, most clever girl in your village? If you can't give Daniel the will to fight, I don't think anyone can.'

The words of the wise animal spirit took root in her soul and her imagination, and from somewhere deep within her, a powerful confidence and purpose began to sprout. Kasheena rose to her feet, and as she did the vision of the lower world began to fade. The ghostly apparition of the turtle also faded, and just before it vanished entirely, Kasheena whispered, 'Thank you.'

The girl stood for a time near the banks of the stream in Daniel's dream world, remembering what she had just seen. She rolled the healing stone in the palm of her hand, absorbing every drop of euphoria the vision of the lower world had planted in her. She had learned the first lesson: to be calm and patient, to think things out before acting. She knew that it would take some time, but she also knew that she would have to consider long and hard as to how best proceed with healing Daniel's spirit.

She never got the chance. Without warning, a tremendous crash of thunder sounded, violently shaking the dreamscape and snapping Kasheena out of her state of altered consciousness. A mad rush of ice-cold wind blasted by her, nearly knocking her to the ground. The skies of the dream world grew dark. Kasheena looked up into black clouds, which seemed to be forming in every direction. The brutal winds of the growing storm were rocking the treetops with tremendous force. Kasheena braced herself against the winds and searched the dreamscape for Daniel, but the boy was nowhere in sight. She began moving slowly toward the spot where she had last seen him. All at once a wind-mixed scream sounded from the distance. It was Daniel! With all the strength she could muster, Kasheena made a mad dash towards the sound of his cry.

Although it seemed impossible, the storm was getting worse. Tremendous flashes of lightning lit up the sky and the accompanying rolls of thunder shook the ground beneath Kasheena's feet as she ran. She picked up her pace. Within minutes, she spied the shaman's staff lying on the ground in front of a large boulder. Daniel was curled up behind the boulder, trying to shelter himself from the storm. As Kasheena reached the boulder, she picked up shaman's staff and fell to her knees beside her friend.

'What's going on?' she shouted.

'It's come for me,' Daniel cried out. 'Death's coming for me and no one can stop it.'

'You have to resist,' Kasheena said without hesitation. She took him by the arm. 'Try. I know it's hard, but you can't give up without

a fight.'

'This isn't your fight.' He pulled himself out of her grip. 'If you don't leave right now, it'll get you, too.'

'I'm not going anywhere,' Kasheena said defiantly. She rose to her feet and brandished the shaman's staff before her. 'I can help you beat this,' she told him, 'But I can't do it alone. You have to believe in yourself and your strength to make it through this. You have to make a stand, and you have to make it right now!'

Daniel looked up at Kasheena from his hiding place behind the boulder. A faint light of hope shone in his eyes. 'You...you really think I can make it through this?'

'No.' Her voice was as strong as stone. 'I don't think you can make it through this. I know you can.'

'You won't leave me? You won't give up on me?'

'Never.' She offered him her free hand. When he touched her fingers, the storm seemed to subside, if only for a moment.

'What do we do now?' Daniel asked as he struggled to his feet.

Kasheena acted instinctively. 'Take this.' She handed him the healing stone. "Hold onto it as tight as you can. Get behind me and ask the spirits for strength and protection.'

Not quite understanding but not daring to disobey, Daniel took the healing stone from Kasheena's hand.

Kasheena turned to face the heart of the storm. 'You can't have him,' she shouted. 'He's mine to watch over and you're not getting him without a fight!'

The storm seemed to understand. It seemed to respond to the girl's challenge. Huge, pitch-black cloud billowed in the skies above; thunder shook the dreamscape like the roaring of an enraged god. A lightning bolt just missed them and splintered the limb of a huge tree, sending it crashing to the ground. Kasheena could see something forming in the center of the tempest, something even blacker than the storm clouds themselves. As the form took shape, it descended toward Kasheena and Daniel. As it approached, it became more defined. Kasheena's heart pounded. She recognized the form. It was a monstrously huge, black hawk. The raptor was so large it seemed to dwarf the storm from which it had come. The hawk swooped with incredible speed.

'Don't look at it.' Kasheena shouted to her friend. 'You have to stay strong. Keep talking to the spirits. Don't give up!'

Obediently, if still fearfully, Daniel turned his back to the bird and the storm. He closed his eyes and held the healing stone to his heart.

The hawk would be on them in a matter of moments. There was nothing else Kasheena could do but stand defiantly between the hawk and her friend, whose life she had sworn to protect. Stiffening her elbows, she held the shaman's staff before her with both hands. As the winds ripped madly at her hair and clothing, the girl wailed a final, rebellious challenge to the advancing raptor.

A pure white snake slithered from beneath the boulder at Kasheena's feet and wrapped itself around her legs. The wings of the death-hawk enshrouded her. The shaman's staff snapped in half and fell to the ground. Kasheena's world faded to black.

Daniel awoke in his bedroom. He looked around dreamily. How long had he been asleep? By the darkness outside his window, he could tell it must be the middle of the night. As his eyes slowly adjusted to the darkness, he saw that he wasn't alone. His doctor was sitting quietly in a chair next to his bed.

'Welcome back, son,' the young doctor said, relief obvious in his voice. 'I thought we were going to lose you for a while there.'

'How long have I been asleep?' Daniel asked.

'Three days.'

'Have you been here the whole time?'

'Yes,' the doctor said, stretching his arms ',I couldn't bring myself to leave you. It's a miracle you're alive. Your fever broke a few hours ago and your heart's been growing stronger. I won't say that you're completely out of the woods yet, but it looks like you've beaten the crisis. You're recovering. I can't explain it.'

'It was that girl.' Daniel gave a mighty yawn. 'She wouldn't let *me give up without a fight.'*

'Girl? What girl are you talking about?' the doctor asked.

'Kasheena. The little girl in my dream. She gave me hope and kept me strong.'

'Well, I don't know anything about any dream girl,' the doctor responded skeptically, 'but your fever was pretty high for a while. Perhaps you were hallucinating. I've never seen anything like this before.'

'I'm still sleepy,' Daniel told the doctor. 'I'm hungry, but If you don't mind, I think I'll go back to sleep for a while. Besides, Kasheena might still be lost somewhere in my dreams. I think I'd better go and look for her.'

'That's fine,' the doctor said with a smile. 'You get all the rest you need. And, oh, by the way, if you run across that little girl in your dreams again, tell her thank you for me.'

'I will,' Daniel replied, and just before he closed his eyes, the boy thought he saw the young doctor's face change into that of an old man. The face looked ancient, worn by time and the sun, but pleasing to look at just the same. A dragonfly flew through an open window in Daniel's bedroom and came to rest on the doctor's shoulder. Daniel began to dream...

The First Tribe

There is a Native American creation myth that tells us the story of *first man and first woman*, whose children peopled the land. There are many variations on the first man-first woman story and the storyline is long, complicated and very difficult to understand. The basic storyline as I understand it begins by telling us of the *first people*. The first people rose up through the three worlds, being banished from each successive world for quarreling. They finally settled in the fourth world, which is the world in which we live today. The story tells of a small group of mysterious beings - sometimes called gods - who attempt to instruct first people by giving them signs, rather than by speaking to them directly. But first people don't understand the signs. After the mysterious beings have departed, first people discuss their visit and try without success to figure out what the signs meant.

So what, you may be asking, does the first man-first woman myth have to do with your own spiritual journey? You may recall that earlier in this book I mentioned following a path that would lead you back to the origin of human spirituality. The time has come to discuss what that origin is, what it means to your quest and how you're going to get there. Just like the *first people*, you must now travel through the worlds to discover and experience this origin for yourself. We go now to visit *first tribe*.

What I am about to suggest is highly speculative and will no doubt spark a great deal of controversy and debate. New concepts, theories and leaps in logic oftentimes do that. Be that as it may, however, it is my contention that at some point in humanity's past, there was a tribe that predated the beginnings of recorded history by millennia, who realized for the very first time that there was something more than just "us." Something larger than the self, and something even larger than the tribe. This something was (and still is) an invisible essence that connected everyone and everything in the universe together. Perhaps they called it *Great Spirit*. It was this essential being, this 'sacred spark' that combined with imagination to give humankind the ability to leap beyond logic and perceive more than we can touch with or hands and see with our eyes. It was this spark of imagination and perception of the unseen that eventually led to the development of human spirituality and religion. Any number of things could have been the trigger for this epiphany. Perhaps a bolt of lightning or the glow of a fire burning far off on the horizon sparked first tribe's awareness of unseen forces. The trigger could have been something as simple as a bird in flight or the stars in the night sky that allowed first tribe to grasp the concept of something more than the tribe could touch and see.

Even though this is fascinating to contemplate, the trigger for the sacred spark of spirituality isn't nearly as important to your spiritual journey as experiencing this sacred spark of realization for yourself. To do so, you will now undertake the next leg of your shamanic travels in which you will lay claim to the second medicine wheel and the pathway that will eventually lead you back through the ages: Back to first tribe.

Tending the Fires Goal Two:
Claiming the Inner Wheel

Here by the campfire's flicker, deep in my blanket curled,
I long for the peace of the pine-gloom, when the scroll of the
lord is unfurled,
And the wind and the wave are silent, and world is
singing to world....
Robert W. Service, *The Three Voices*

Peruvian shamans believe in what are known as *The Three Worlds*, which are the *overworld*, the *middle world*, and the *lower world*. The overworld is believed to be inhabited by spiritual beings, the middle world by humans, animals, and plants, and the lower world by power animals and helpful animal spirits. Thus far in her story, Kasheena has visited the middle world (in dreams at least), where she learned some valuable lessons about herself and her quest to become a shaman. Now that you are ready to undertake the second leg of your spiritual journey, it is time to begin discussing these three worlds so that you can learn to speak their languages. This is known as *speaking with the three voices*

In the first leg of your spiritual journey you traveled into the spirit lands where you laid claim to the first medicine wheel. The spirit lands should be considered an area of claimed spiritual space where the three worlds overlap, thus allowing the spirit lands to be inhabited by any combination of entities from any or all of the three worlds. I explained to you earlier in this book that your spirit lands could possibly be populated by any number of tribes, shamans, plants, animals, animal spirits, or spiritual beings. Although there is much you can learn by simply spending time investigating your spirit lands and interacting with its inhabitants, to learn to speak with the three voices you must immerse yourself in each of the three worlds and experience them first-hand. You will begin your journey into the three worlds by traveling to the lower world, where you will lay claim to the second medicine wheel. This is the world of power animals and helpful animal spirits.

The goal of your second journey into the spirit lands is threefold.

One - To make improvements and add embellishments to your base camp, which is located near the first medicine wheel.

Two - To travel through the gateway of the first medicine wheel, enter into the lower world, and lay claim to the second medicine wheel.

Three - To make contact with some of the power animals and helpful animal spirits that inhabit the lower world and attempt to enlist their aid in assisting you in your spiritual quest.

Before you get started on the second leg of your journey, let's take a closer look at these three goals. I have a few suggestions and lessons that might just come in handy.

Improving Your Base Camp

There are two main reasons why it's a good idea to take the time to make improvements to your base camp. First, the more appealing your base camp is, the more likely you will be eager to spend more time in it. Second, a well-equipped base camp may very well be appealing to some of the inhabitants of the spirit lands and might prompt some of the inhabitants to pay you a visit. You may find these visits to be educational and entertaining. Your base camp should be viewed as a temporary home in the spirit lands and should contain everything you need for spiritual comfort and enjoyment. Just like an earthly campsite, a well-equipped base camp should be capable of providing you refuge and sanctuary in the spirit lands.

An easy way to decide how best to equip your base camp in the spirit lands is to consider how you would equip a campsite here on mundane earth. Do you enjoy sitting around a campfire? If so, then create one in your base camp. Would you use torches at a campsite? How about a tent or even a teepee? Would you take a drum or another musical instrument with you to an earthly campsite? If so, your base camp in the spirit lands should be stocked with these things as well. The point is that you should have everything you need for comfort and enjoyment while spending time in the spirit lands, the only difference being that instead of being physical, the items you use to furnish your base camp will be mental, spiritual, and visual. You can either visualize yourself bringing any desired items with you as you enter into the spirit lands from the earthly plane, or (better) create them yourself once you've arrived. You can also see if there might be any friendly inhabitants in the spirit lands that would be willing to gift you with them. Get creative and have some fun with the process. Make it a meaningful personal experience. After all, it's *your* base camp.

Entering the Lower World and Claiming the Second Medicine Wheel

On your next journey into the spirit lands, your goal is to enter the gateway of the first medicine wheel and lay claim to the second, or inner medicine wheel. By traveling through the first gateway, you will essentially be entering into what is known as the lower world. What the lower world will look and feel like to you is impossible for me to predict. The lower world could appear to you as a beautiful meadow or a great underground cavern. It could be located high atop a mountain or deep in a valley. No matter where the lower world is located for you, the second medicine wheel should be close by and relatively easy to find.

Locating and investigating the second medicine wheel is without question one of the most important aspects of the second leg of your spiritual journey. One the spokes of the second medicine wheel is the pathway that will lead you back through time to first tribe. Once the second medicine wheel has been located, your next task will be to walk the perimeter of the wheel, investigating each of the spokes as you go along. Once you've found the spoke that's right for your journey, the vision of a Great Tribe will appear before you. This tribe should be considered a spiritual family of sort and once you've made contact with this tribe (which you will do on your third journey into the spirit lands), the tribe will unconditionally accept you as one of their own. Instructions for working with the second medicine wheel will be outlined in detail later on in this chapter.

Working With the Animal Spirits That Inhabit the Lower World

You may recall that power animals and helpful animal spirits populate the lower world. Making contact with some of these animal spirits is the third goal of your second journey into the spirit lands. Although working with the animal spirits of the lower world may not seem as important to your spiritual journey as working with the Great Tribe, animal spirits can be extremely helpful to your quest. They can teach you many valuable lessons about yourself and the lower world. Working with animal spirits is a highly personal experience and the technique that works best for you might not work well for another individual. My good friend and author, Carol Rosinski, has worked with animal spirits for many years and the following basic techniques for working with animal spirits were inspired by her wonderful teachings.

There is no single way for working with animal spirits that's right for everyone. You may need to do some experimenting before you succeed. Some people are visual, some are tactile, some are verbal, and some are a combination. No matter how you are doing the work, the key is to allow the animal spirit to lead you. You do not lead it. Allow the animal spirit to lead you to where it feels you need to go instead of suggesting a destination.

To begin working with animal spirits, find a nice comfortable spot in the lower world, relax your mind and imagine all of the different types of animals you might encounter. After a time, one or more spirit animals may take interest in you (if they haven't already) and approach you. Once an animal spirit has made contact, speak to it of your spiritual quest and ask the animal spirit if it would be willing to assist you. If you are a visual person, ask the animal spirit to take you on a visual journey. If you are a verbal person, ask the animal spirit to tell you a story, or simply ask it to tell you what it feels you need to know. If you are a tactile person, the journey the animal spirit takes you on may involve touching the animal or tracking it by following its scent or the sounds that it makes. No matter what the animal spirit tells you or where it leads you, properly thank the animal spirit for its time before it leaves. Do this even if you don't understand what you were told or shown by the animal spirit. Working with animal spirits takes time, practice and patience. It is not unusual for an animal spirit to show or tell you the same thing several times before you understand the message it is trying to relay to you.

That just about sums up everything you need to know about the three goals of the second leg of your spiritual journey. Later on in this chapter, I will provide you with a few guided visualizations that will hopefully enhance your second journey. If you are ready, allow me to guide your first few steps into the spirit lands where you will enter the lower world and lay claim to the second medicine wheel: the vehicle that will lead you to the Great Tribe and back through the ages to experience the first sacred spark of human spirituality.

Shamanic Traveling Path Two:
The Descending

Preparation and technique for your second adventure in shamanic traveling will be the same as they were for your first adventure. If you don't recall the preparations and technique necessary for shamanic traveling, refer to the instructions and guidelines located on page 25 of this book to refresh your memory. Before you begin the second leg of your journey, you will need to contemplate any changes or additions you wish to make to your base camp in the spirit lands. If you plan to carry items for your base camp with you from the mundane plane, preparation for your second journey will vary slightly from the usual preparation. If you choose to carry the items with you, after you have prepared your shamanic room and are ready to begin your journey, you will need to meditate on the base camp, and, as clearly as you are able, visualize the items and imagine yourself carrying them with you as you enter into the spirit lands. Other than that, the preparation and technique for shamanic traveling will remain the same.

Once you have entered into the spirit lands, spend some time looking around to see if the spirit lands have changed since your last visit. The spirit lands will most likely be different each time you enter them. They change because each time you visit them, you will be imprinting more and more of yourself and your energy onto the spirit lands and their inhabitants. Once you have thoroughly investigated the spirit lands, your next order of business is to attend to your base camp. If you have brought the desired items with you from the mundane plane, you can head directly to your base camp and make the desired changes. If you decided to create or find the items in the spirit lands, you will need to attend to that task before heading to your base camp. Either way, once the changes and additions have been made, spend some time relaxing in your base camp and see if your presence in the camp attracts any visitors. Who or what shows up just may surprise you.

Your next order of business is to enter the gateway of the first medicine wheel and descend to the lower world. You will want to make the descent a magical and meaningful experience. To do so, stand before the gateway of the first medicine wheel and imagine the wonders that lie ahead of you. Feel the energies of the spirit lands as they flow all around you. Feel the power of the medicine wheel, and know without question that this power exists within you as well. Believe with all your heart and soul that the journey and the lower world will be wondrous beyond imagination. Step into the gateway of the medicine wheel. Feel the doorway to the lower world opening before you. Cross the threshold and feel yourself softly and slowly descending into the lower world.

How the lower world will look and feel to you is impossible for me to predict but I have little doubt that it will be everything you had hoped for. It may even exceed your expectations. You may very well be excited about the prospect of exploring the lower world in depth but keep in mind that you still have several major tasks ahead on your journey. Feel free to look around a bit, but don't expend too much of your spiritual energy. You don't want to exhaust yourself before meeting your goals. If the second medicine wheel isn't within sight, you will need to locate it. If you are having trouble finding the second medicine wheel, be still and see if you can pick up on the medicine wheel's energy pattern. There will be no mistaking its power.

Once you have located the second medicine wheel, spend some time acquainting yourself with how the medicine wheel looks and feels. Experience the wheel's energy and try to pick up on what you can see with your inner eyes and touch with your inner hands. The spokes of the second medicine wheel are capable of carrying you anywhere you wish to travel. You can experience the possibilities of the second medicine wheel to their extent at a later time, but for now you have a specific goal to meet: To find the Great Tribe.

To find the Great Tribe, stand before the second medicine wheel. Speaking aloud or in your imagination, clearly state your purpose and intention. Now slowly walk the perimeter of the wheel and closely examine each spoke of the wheel as you go along. Imagine the Great Tribe as you walk. Visualize the Great Tribe in your mind. Imagine what it would be like to be a member of this tribe. Imagine all of the people that belong to the Great Tribe: the children and the elderly, the shamans and the chieftains, the hunters and the warriors. Build the vision of the Great Tribe until you can see it clearly in your mind. Build the vision until you can hear the voices of the tribe and you can smell the scents of land in air. Build the vision until a spoke on the medicine wheel begins to change, opening a pathway before you. Build the vision until you can feel the Great Tribe all around you. Look deep within the vision of the pathway and behold the Great Tribe.

You can now spend as much time as you wish watching the members of the Great Tribe and experiencing their energies. However, *under no circumstances should you attempt to interact with the tribal members or enter the pathway of the second medicine wheel at this time.* Doing so would greatly compromise my ability to lead you to the ultimate goal of your shamanic travels, which is to eventually stand with the Great Tribe as they experience the first sacred spark of human spirituality.

After you have spent a meaningful amount of time experiencing the vision of the Great Tribe, move away from the medicine wheel until the vision begins to fade. Once the vision has faded away into nothingness, thank the spirits for guiding you and return to the gateway that led you into the lower world. You now have a choice to make. Depending on how much energy you have expended thus far, you can return to the spirit lands and then move onward to the earthly plane, or you can spend a bit more time in the lower world and attempt to make contact with the animal spirits that dwell there. Keep in mind that you can do so at a later time, and that if you've overextended yourself there's absolutely no reason to push it. The spirit lands and the medicine wheels will be at your disposal for as long as you desire them to be a part of your present and future spiritual journey. If you decide to remain in the lower world and make contact with the animal spirits, remember to follow the guidelines for doing so that I offered you earlier in this chapter.

When you are ready to return to your regular earthly existence, enter the pathway that leads back to the spirit lands and look for a soft glow of light somewhere in the distance. This light is the candle burning in your room on the earthly plane. Locate and follow along the path that leads to the candlelight until it becomes so bright in your eyes and in your mind that you can see nothing else. Open your eyes and you will have returned to the earthly plane.

The fires of your spirituality have grown ever higher. A pathway that leads to the Great Tribe is now yours for the taking. Make some time this evening to rest and revel in the experience of your second adventure. But don't get too comfy; the time of your third journey is nearly at hand.

Emergence Part Three:
Darkness, Darkness

Kasheena awoke to flickering firelight and the smell of fresh herbs. How long had she been asleep? She didn't know for sure, but judging by the stiffness in her arms and legs, it must have been a very long time. Raising her head, she saw that she was lying inside a large cavern near a campfire. She also saw that she wasn't alone. Sitting across the fire from her was a plump old woman with dark skin and white hair. The woman seemed to be busily working at some task. Rising to her feet so she could get a better look, Kasheena saw that the woman, who had a white snake painted on her arm, was grinding plants in a turtle shell. Kasheena stretched, let out a mighty yawn, and walked around the fire toward the old woman.

'Hello, Grandmother,' she said respectfully. 'My name's Kasheena. I think I'm lost again. Can you please tell me where I am?'

When the old woman looked up at her with a broad smile, Kasheena saw that a bandage covered her left eye. 'Curious, Child,' the old woman replied, 'that you don't know where you are. After everything you've been through, I would have thought you'd have that figured out by now.'

'Wh - what do you mean?' Kasheena asked. 'How could I possibly know where I am? I keep waking up in strange places I've never even seen before. Everyone talks to me in riddles. Nobody will tell me what's happening to me.'

As she spoke, Kasheena suddenly noticed that something about herself had changed. Her voice didn't quite sound right. Her body felt different. She stretched her arms out before her and looked down at her body. Yes, she could see differences. She was much older than she had been before she had lost consciousness! How could this be? She had blacked-out in Daniel's dream world as a little girl and had somehow awakened in this cavern a young woman. Kasheena fell to her knees next to the old woman and gently touched her arm.

'Grandmother, please tell me what has happened to me. I - I've somehow grown older. Have I grown up?'

The old woman smiled. 'You certainly shouldn't be surprised by that. It happens to everyone if they're lucky.'

'But I don't understand! How did it happen so quickly?'

'Child, who knows these things?' The old woman set the shell full of herbs on the ground next to the fire. 'You might as well ask me why the sun comes up every morning or why the sky is blue. From your perspective, you've only just arrived at this place. From another perspective, you may have been here a very long time. Who's to say for sure?'

Kasheena slowly raised one hand and gently brought it to rest on the side of the old woman's face.

Tell me, Grandmother, how did you injure your eye?'

'Why, it's not injured at all, Child. Its sight has only been taken from me for a time. It was the price I paid for helping you. I made a choice and that's that. Nothing to be done for it now, I'm afraid.'

Kasheena stared at the white snake on the old woman's arm. Something about it seemed familiar. Suddenly her mind flooded with memories, and realization hit home.

'The snake in Daniel's dream world...,' she murmured under her breath, speaking more to herself than to the old woman. Then she looked at the old woman again. 'It was you, wasn't it? Just before the hawk took me...I remember seeing you. You did something to me, didn't you? Somehow...somehow you protected me from the raptor.'

'I only did for you what you did for the boy. Nothing more, nothing less.'

'He's alive? Daniel survived the hawk's attack?'

'Yes, Child. He's alive. But, like you, he's undergone a few changes. Let's just say...well, let's say he's different than he was before and leave it at that. Our time together is running short, and *there are a few things I must discuss with you before he arrives.'*

'Before who arrives, Grandmother? Daniel?'

'Why no, Child. Death, of course.'

Daniel awoke in the village of the great tribe with a horrible taste in his mouth. Whatever the chieftain had given him to drink the night before was the foulest tasting stuff imaginable, but it had taken him months to gain the chieftain's trust, and he hadn't wanted to offend him by refusing. Daniel immediately went about the task of tidying up his campsite. It felt as though he'd been waiting his entire life for this day to arrive and he wanted everything about it to be perfect. He rolled and tied his sleeping bag, then rinsed out his coffee pot and cup. Tonight the shaman would take him to a secret place and speak with him of his medicine. At long last, the mysteries of healing the spirit would be revealed to him.

Daniel had spent the last fifteen years of his life learning how to heal the human body. He had become a fine doctor and took great pleasure in his ability to cure people's ills. But even with everything that he had learned and accomplished in medical school, he still felt that something was missing. There was an emptiness inside him that only learning the ways of healing the spirit would fill. He had been inspired to study medicine after inexplicably surviving a childhood illness that in all logic should have ended his life. On the night of his brush with death, he had awakened from a strange dream in which he had encountered a young girl who encouraged him to fight his illness and make a stand against death. Even though it had been only a dream, in some way he couldn't quite understand or explain, he felt as though he owed his very life to the girl and that even the path of the spirit he would walk tonight was somehow due to her intervention. If only he could remember her name....

A chill ran down Kasheena's spine. The firelight vanished as the last wisps of flame died to embers. The cavern was soundless and still. It almost seemed as though the cavern itself were quietly waiting for someone to arrive.

'What do you mean by 'he' Grandmother? Are you telling me that death is a person? Is that what you're telling me?' It was suddenly so dark that she could hardly see the woman sitting before her.

'A part of him is, of course, Child. But like you and me, there is much more to him than can be seen with the eye. In the dream world, he appeared to you as a hawk. He chose a form you could understand, a form your mind would accept. In this world, he will take on another form, one even more frightening than the hawk, I expect.'

'So he means to take me? He means to end my life?' Kasheena's lips trembled as she spoke.

The old woman took Kasheena's hands and she pulled her forward, cradling her in her arms. 'Hush, Child,' she whispered. 'He won't harm you directly at this time. There are rules he must follow, laws that cannot be broken without great consequence. But you must understand that by coming between him and the boy you have altered the natural course of things. You have stood between the predator and the prey, and a price must be paid for such inter-vention. I don't know what he intends for you, but I know that no matter what it is, you're strong enough to survive it.'

Kasheena wiped the tears from her face and looked deeply into the old woman's unbandaged eye. "What are you, Grandmother?" she asked, "Please tell me."

'I'm old, Child. I'm very old and very tired, but there's a bit of magic left in me yet.' She allowed herself a brief smile. 'You must go deep into the cavern,' she said, 'And seek him out. Don't wait for him to come looking for you. He already knows how brave you are, and if you seek him out he will hold your bravery in high regard.' Another narrow smile. 'He might go a bit easier on you than he would have otherwise. I don't know what awaits you in the shadows, Child, but I do know that he's prepared this place for you. This place is between the worlds, not on one side or the other, but *somewhere in middle, like the threshold of a doorway.'*

'I have to face him alone?'

'Yes, Child.' Now the old woman merely sighed. 'Where you're going, I cannot follow. Helping you the first time cost me dear, dearer than you know. I can't risk any further loss of my sight. I have other children to look after. As I looked after you.'

Kasheena smiled at the old woman, 'You see much more with your one eye than I do with both of mine.'

'Oh, I think you see just fine.'

Without another word, she filled a small pouch with the herbs she had ground in the turtle shell and fastened it around Kasheena's neck with a leather strap. She then picked up a small jar filled with a thick white paste and, lifting Kasheena's dress, drew a snake on her belly with her fingers. 'That'll just be our little secret,' she said with a sly grin. Finally, she put the empty turtle shell into Kasheena's hands. 'You'd best be on your way, Child.'

Now Kasheena recognized the shell. It was the one her animal spirit had left for her in Daniel's dream world. Being able to hold the shell again brought her comfort. Taking a few cautious steps into the corridor past the cavern, she asked, 'How will I see where I'm going?'

There was no response.

In the dim light of the last dying embers of the campfire, Kasheena saw a pure white snake slither away into the darkness. She took a deep breath and exhaled it with a great sigh. The question was irrelevant. She would see exactly what he wanted her to see, nothing more, nothing less. With seemingly no other choice, Kasheena walked into the blackness of the corridor.

The shaman had been gazing into the fire for what seemed like hours. He hadn't so much as moved or spoken the entire time. Daniel was starting to get impatient, but he knew that he dared not show it. The shaman would undoubtedly judge everything he said and did. If he blew the opportunity to learn the ways of the spirit medicine now, he might not ever get another chance. It was already well past nightfall. Daniel was beginning to wonder if the shaman intended to teach him anything tonight.

After what seemed like an eternity of waiting, the shaman at last rose to his feet and motioned Daniel to his side.

'Are we ready to go now, Great Father?' Daniel's enthusiasm was clear in his voice. A huge smile came over the shaman's face and without speaking a word he produced a small flask from under his coat and handed it to Daniel. Daniel's heart sank into his stomach. He suddenly felt nauseous. Not again. He fought back the urge to cringe. 'Do you want me to drink this?' he asked, already knowing the answer.

The shaman lifted his hand to his mouth and made a loud popping sound with his tongue.

'That must be shaman for "bottoms up,"' Daniel thought as he uncorked the flask and brought it to his lips. The stuff the chieftain had given him to drink the night before had tasted awful, but whatever was in the shaman's flask was much, much worse. The smell alone had almost made him gag, and it took every ounce of willpower he could summon to force the shaman's brew down his gullet.

With the business of downing the drink over, the shaman patted Daniel on the back in approval and took the flask from his hand. 'We must go now,' he said in voice that verged on being apologetic. 'The spirits have made us wait longer than I had hoped, but it is they who set the pace, not you or I. They have shown me that there is another who walks the path of the spirit this night, one whose journey parallels your own. The path she will walk is the path of darkness. The spirits have shown me that your path will intersect with hers.' He looked into Daniel's eyes. 'Let us hope that the path the spirits have chosen for you is the path of light.' He buttoned the collar of his coat and motioned for Daniel to follow him.

Carefully considering the shaman's words, Daniel hesitated, but only for a moment. He turned to the fire, thinking that bringing along a torch to light their way might not be a bad idea. Then, thinking better of it, he sighed and turned his back to the fire. Torchlight was irrelevant, and he knew it. Tonight he would see exactly what the spirits wanted him to see, nothing more, nothing less. Uncertain what awaited him, Daniel followed the shaman into the night.

The walls of the corridor felt cold and unforgiving under Kasheena's hands. Without a light, she would have to feel her way along the walls. She was trying her best to be courageous but she couldn't keep from imagining all of the horrible things that might be waiting for her in the bowels of the cavern. Terrible things, unspeakable things. She desperately wanted to be back in the arms of the old woman. She wanted to be somewhere safe and warm where nothing could harm her. She wanted to be back home with her tribe. Tears welled in her eyes, but this time she managed to fight them back. Escaping the cavern hinged on her ability to remain brave. She would have to keep moving.

As Daniel paced behind the shaman, he began to have strange visions. He was seeing things he couldn't explain. He saw an old woman with dark skin and white hair who suddenly changed into a pure white snake that slithered away in the darkness. He saw a powerful warrior spirit with glowing eyes and huge bird's wings. The warrior spirit let out a defiant cry before fading away into nothingness. He saw an old shaman and a young girl standing on the crown of a steep hill. He saw a young woman desperately clawing her way through a dark tunnel. He saw a tribe mourning the passing of a great elder.

Daniel couldn't tell if he was seeing these visions with his eyes or his imagination. Even though what he saw looked real, it also seemed almost ghostlike, like he was seeing glimpses of other times and other places. 'Exactly what was it you gave me to drink?' he muttered, knowing full well the effects that alcohol and narcotic substances have on the mind. The visions faded as quickly as they had come, and after several more minutes of walking, Daniel could see the welcome light of torches burning on the path ahead. He also saw where the shaman had led him: the tribal burial grounds.

Kasheena heard something rustling around her in the darkness. Or was it just her mind playing tricks on her? Her heart began to race, but she stood motionless and silent in the dark corridor. If something really was nearby, she didn't want to tip it off to her location. She heard the rustling noise again. This time it was much closer. Suddenly, her nose filled with a pungent odor. Her eyes and nostrils started to sting. After a few moments, she realized that the odor was coming form the pouch of herbs the old woman had tied around her neck. The smell was almost unbearable. She untied the leather strap, knelt down, and set the pouch on the ground at her feet. When something brushed her arm in the darkness, she let out a shriek. To make matters worse, the turtle shell slipped from her hand and hit the ground with a crashing sound that echoed in the darkness.

Even though the tribal burial ground was a place of death, Daniel found it beautiful, almost enchanting. He knelt down, scooped up a pinch of earth and gently rolled it in the palm of his hand, allowing the broken pieces of dirt to sift through his fingers. 'Father,' he said to the shaman, 'I feel a presence here. I feel as though I'm in the company of the tribe's great ancestors. I can almost see their faces and hear their voices. Is that what you brought me here to experience?'

As the shaman turned, the look in his eyes was so foreboding it sent a chill down Daniel's spine. 'We are in the midst of the ancestors,' the shaman replied. 'That is true. You have done well to sense their presence. But it is not they who have awaited your arrival this night. I had hoped your first lesson would have been easier, less intense than what you must face. But always it is our

63

own heart, the fears of our own spirit that must be overcome if we are to learn to heal the spirits of others. This is always the first lesson. There is no way around it'

The shaman turned away from Daniel and looked hard into the shadows. He pulled his coat more tightly across his chest and took several cautious steps backward. 'I must go now,' he said, his eyes never leaving the shadows. 'I will return for you at first light. I will be prepared to attend to you. May the presence of the ancestors give you strength, may the breath of the Great Spirit not blow on you as bitterly as I fear it will.' And without another word, the shaman turned away and disappeared into the darkness.

Daniel was more than a little troubled by his words. 'What did you see in the shadows?' he asked, his breath a ghostly mist in the chilly night air, but the shaman was already gone. He peered deep into the darkness, hoping to catch a glimpse of what the shaman had been staring at so intently. He saw nothing. Suddenly, he felt a presence behind him. He turned sharply to face it and nearly lost his footing in the soft earth. The warrior was huge, perhaps the largest man Daniel had ever seen. A black hawk was painted on his chest.

Kasheena didn't dare to move. The darkness that had vexed her was now her only ally in staying hidden from whatever was stalking her. She listened carefully for the sound of anything moving. Nothing. As cautiously as she could, she knelt down and felt around for the turtle shell. She located it quickly, but just as she was picking it up, something brushed her arm. Her breath seized in her chest. She was more frightened than she had ever been before. Her mind raced with terrifying images, she imagined all kinds of awful creatures crawling toward her in the black cavern, things that he had sent - or brought with him - to torment her. A scratching sound reverberated through the darkness. Kasheena could no longer resist her instinct. She snatched up the shell, sprang to her feet and ran blindly down the corridor.

Daniel stared up at the enormous man with caution. Something about him felt familiar but in a way that was alarming. 'Do I know you?' he asked. 'Are you a warrior from the village?'

The man stared down at Daniel with eyes that seemed to see into his very soul. A hint of a smile came to the man's lips. He began circling Daniel like a predator cornering its prey.

'We have met once before,' he finally replied, 'But it was a very long time ago. And, no, you do not know me, at least not yet. I am no warrior. I am more like what you would call a hunter.' He paused. 'I am a collector of things.'

'Exactly what is it that you hunt?' Daniel asked, fearing he already knew the answer.

'Tonight I hunt you.'

Kasheena tripped in the darkness and she came crashing down on the floor of the corridor. A sharp pain surged through her le, but she ignored it and scrambled back up to her feet. Certain that whatever was chasing her was closing in, she kept running. The scratching sound seemed to be all around her now. She could no longer tell if it was coming from behind her or somewhere out in front. As she ran, Kasheena began doubting her ability to confront her captor. She began doubting she would make it out of the cavern at all.

Suddenly something changed. She was running on dirt, running up an incline. Had she left the cavern? She couldn't tell. All she could do was keep running. The further she ran, the softer and deeper the dirt became. The incline quickly became so steep that she had no other choice but to drop to her hands and knees and climb.

As the man circled, Daniel turned with him, afraid to take his eyes off the stranger for even a second. 'What do you mean you're hunting me?' he asked, trying to keep his voice even. 'People don't hunt other people.'

The huge man just smiled and kept circling. Daniel felt as though he were being sized up. He didn't care for how that felt.

'I will give you a choice,' the man said. 'A choice your ally doesn't have. You can face me or walk away. If you choose to face me, it will mean your end. If you choose to walk away, you will be allowed to leave unharmed but it will mean abandoning your quest to learn the ways of the spirit medicine. It will also mean leaving the girl to my mercy. Make your choice. Make it now.'

'Ally? Girl? What the hell are you talking about?' Daniel was completely confused. He felt as though he were on trial for a crime he was unaware of committing. He began questioning the rationality of his decision to seek out the tribe and the shaman in the first place.

She clawed frantically at the dirt. She was practically buried it now and it took all the strength and willpower she could summon just to inch her way up the hill. Whatever was pursuing her was close behind, of that she was certain. No matter how difficult the climb became, she would have to keep moving. She still held the turtle shell, even though dragging it along was a cumbersome chore. Her instincts told had her that she would need it to escape the cavern. Her instincts were right. As she reached forward, Kasheena could feel that the corridor ahead was completely blocked. There was only one-way to escape the cavern. She would have to dig.

'Fine!' Daniel practically shouted at the man, angered by his words and the situation. 'I don't need this crap and I certainly don't appreciate being threatened. I came here to learn how to help people, not to be bullied by a complete stranger. And as far as this girl is concerned, I don't know what the hell you're talking about. We'll just see what the shaman has to say about all this.'

The man just stared at Daniel. He was no longer smiling.

She scooped furiously at the dirt with the shell, pushing it behind her and kicking it back with her feet. She knew that if she stopped for even a moment, she would lose hope and stop digging. And if she stopped digging, she was as good as dead. Her arms were getting tired and the pain in her leg was getting worse. If she didn't break free soon, she would be buried alive in the dirt.

'If that is your decision,' the man replied in a cold, emotionless voice, 'you may leave unharmed as I have promised. But it is unwise to anger me. I have made a great sacrifice for you and the girl. My sacrifice has left its mark upon me. If you leave, you must carry my mark as well.'

The warrior stroked the hawk painted on his chest with his fingertips. He reached out. Touching Daniel's cheek, he drew a line with the paint on his fingers.

Suddenly Daniel's head began to swim. Everything around him started to change. The visions were returning.

She shoveled madly at the dirt, thrusting herself forward with her legs and feet as she opened a slim passage. It was getting harder and harder to breathe. She was almost out of time. She kept digging.

The enormous man's eyes began to glow. He sprouted a pair of monstrous black hawk's wings that moved ominously in the air above him. The painting of the hawk on his chest started to change. The black pigment seemed to swirl and flow as though it were alive.

The lack of oxygen was playing tricks on her mind. She was having strange visions. She saw a shaman and an enormous bird of prey engaged in battle. She saw a tribe mourning the passing of a great elder. She saw herself as a strong and beautiful woman, standing among windswept pines at the top of a steep hill. She could almost feel the breeze on her face.

The swirling pigment on the man's chest seemed to create a picture. It was a valley with billowing clouds above it, a wide stream flowing through it. The picture was moving. It looked like a living landscape.

She gasped for breath. She was almost out of air, the dirt was closing *in, and it was far too late to turn back. She kept digging.*

The clouds in the picture turned pitch-black. A strong wind began to blow. The sky flashed with lightning, and the valley was rocked by tremendous crashes of thunder.

She could no longer breathe. She was losing consciousness. Somehow, she kept digging.

Something was forming in the center of the tempest, something even blacker than the storm clouds themselves

Her mind filled with memories of her village and her tribe. She remembered that she had promised to gather firewood for her grandmother the day she had followed the shaman to the top of the hill. She hadn't gotten around to doing it. She kept digging.

Daniel recognized the form.
    Digging…
    His heart pounded in his chest…
    Digging…
    The raptor…
    Digging…
    The little girl…
    Digging…
    Kasheena…
    Digging…
    Her hand broke the surface of the ground. With the last remnants of whatever strength she possessed, she freed herself from the earth and emerged, gasping for breath.

He looked up at the man in horror. The man looked normal, again, no longer a winged demon with a living picture on his chest. But Daniel knew who this apparition really was. 'No,' he muttered, 'it's not possible.' He knew he was trying to talk himself out of what he knew to be true. 'It's just not possible. That's all there is to it. The shaman drugged me...he, he had to have. It's the only rational explanation.'

Rational or not, it wasn't the only explanation, and he knew it. He remembered the dream fully now. For the first time since he was a little boy, he remembered the dream: Every facet, every detail. The birdman was neither bird nor man, but something else: Something impossible.

She lay flat on her back, exhausted and in agony. She breathed in huge lungfuls of oxygen, exhaling into the chilly night air in a mist. She hadn't the slightest idea where she was, but for the moment that didn't matter. She was alive. Alive and free of the cavern, free from the dirt. That was all that mattered. She would just lie here for a few moments, catching her breath and gazing at the stars in the night sky.

Once her breathing had slowed to something resembling normal, she rolled on her side, wincing at the pain in her leg. 'What am I seeing?' she asked herself out loud. 'Where am I?' She had visited burial grounds many times with her grandmother but this one was unfamiliar to her. It was unlike anything she had ever seen. The burial mounds were funny shaped and arranged in strange patterns. Many of the marker stones were engraved with symbols that she didn't recognize. The altars and totems appeared to represent many different tribes. There seemed to be no order, no sense to the anything she could see.

Finding the strength to sit up, she finally pushed herself to her knees and looked at the ground she had been laying on. She had emerged into the burial grounds through a grave. The marker stone at the foot of the grave was carved with a glyph of a hawk.

He was more frightened than he had ever been in his life. He wanted to run, to get away from the enormous man and what his presence in the burial ground meant. But he had a question that he simply had to know the answer to. From somewhere deep inside himself, he summoned the courage to ask it. 'The girl...Kasheena...where is she? What have you done with her?'

'Why, Great Healer,' the man answered in an ordinary voice, as though he was bewildered by the question, 'She is right here. Can you not see her? Can you not hear her voice and feel her presence?'

"Wh - what?' Daniel was starting to feel light-headed again.

For a second time, the warrior touched him on the face. As his fingertips came to rest on Daniel's cheek, the man's left eye slowly faded from black to gray and then to pure white.

Daniel felt as though he was rising up and out of his body. His hands and arms began to tingle. Suddenly, he was seeing things again. Apparitions. Ghostlike forms floating across the burial ground. He could hear their whispered voices.

All at once, he saw her. She was older than she had been in his dream, but there was no mistaking her. It was the girl who had given him strength and encouraged him to fight his illness. She was wrapped in the coils of a huge, white snake.

Ignoring the pain in her leg, Kasheena scurried off the burial mound and brushed the dirt from her hair and dress. The thought of having climbed through a grave sickened her. She snatched the turtle shell from the ground and was turning away from the grave when something caught her eye. A soft glow of firelight at the far end of the burial ground. Uncertain, but unable to overcome her own curiosity, she slowly made her way toward the light.

As she neared the fire, she was delighted to see that the old woman was sitting on the ground before it, warming her hands. She was just about to call out a greeting when a strong feeling of warning washed over her. Something was wrong, something was out of place. Was this really what she had expected to see? The old woman sitting by a cozy fire as though nothing at all unusual had happened? Hadn't she expected to see him instead? And what about the pouch of herbs? She touched her throat where the pouch had lain.

'Why would the old woman tie something around my neck that would make my eyes and nose sting? Was she trying to poison me?'

She couldn't answer any of her own questions. But she was determined to find out what was happening.

As the birdman removed his fingers from Daniel's cheek, his eye instantly changed from white to black. Daniel rubbed at his face, trying to shake off the terrible feelings that the vision of Kasheena had manifested inside him. The birdman had her trapped, he was sure, imprisoned somewhere just beyond this world, somewhere just beyond his understanding. Even though much of what was happening was beyond his comprehension, in some inexplicable way it seemed to make sense.

'We've come full circle, haven't we?' *Daniel thought, his mind grasping at the last few pieces of the answer.* 'The last time we met, you were my champion. My defender. I wouldn't even be here right now if it wasn't for you. I'd be somewhere with...' *He drew in a deep breath and stared up at the birdman, who returned his stare.* 'So,' *he said,* 'your bargain still stands? If I face you in combat, you'll spare the girl's life? You'll show her mercy? Set her free?'

'Of course my bargain still stands.' *His adversary sounded offended by the very nature of the question.*

'Then I've changed my mind,' *Daniel said without hesitation.* 'I choose to face you.'

'Good.' *The enormous man smiled.* 'It is settled. The terms of my bargain haven't changed.' *He smiled again.* 'But I never said anything about combat. I never said that I would harm the girl. Facing me is far worse than any battle you can imagine. Facing me is a battle that cannot be won, only endured. And as far as the girl is concerned, Healer, she is no more my prisoner than you are. The two of you have made your own decisions, chosen your own paths. No one has chosen them for you. No, Healer, I am not the architect

71

of your prisons. You and the girl carry that responsibility. I am merely the key to unlocking their doors.'

'I...I don't understand.' Daniel was completely confused. 'You said that facing you would mean my end. You said that if I walked away it meant leaving the girl at your mercy.'

'The word "end" has many meanings, Healer. End can mean death and ruin. It can also mean the furthermost point imaginable. Mercy is also ambiguous. It can be an act of kindness, the divine favor of the Great Spirit itself. But all of that is irrelevant now. The choice has been made and there is no turning back. Tonight you will face me and in as much you will also be facing yourself. You will confront your deepest fears and endure the darkness of your own spirit. Tonight you will travel to the furthermost point imaginable and unravel the mystery of your destiny. Tonight, you will meet your end.'

'Hello, Grandmother,' Kasheena called out warily. 'What are you doing here?,'' And,' she asked without speaking ' exactly where is here?'

'Well hello, Child!' A broad smile came over the old woman's round face. 'Come and sit with me by the fire.' She beckoned. 'Fire is a good friend to have on such a cold night. Besides, I could use some company.'

Kasheena walked cautiously toward the fire and chose a spot that was close enough to the old woman that she could see and hear her clearly but far enough away to feel comfortable. The warmth of the fire felt good on her cold skin and Kasheena sat in silence for a time, watching the old woman through the haze of dancing smoke and flame. As she became warmer, Kasheena thought about what she'd experienced in the cavern. She considered the rest of her journey as well.'Is this just another dream?' she wondered. She recalled what the old shaman had said to her the night she had followed him to the top of the hill, a night that seemed an eternity ago. ' Is this where the spirits meant to bring me? Or did I get lost somewhere along the way?' *She somehow knew that the answers were close at hand, dangling just beyond her grasp. She was about to ask the old woman how they had ended up in the burial ground when she noticed something else - the old woman's left eye was no longer bandaged.*

'Grandmother,' *she ventured,* 'is your eye better now?' *Although she was still suspicious of the old woman, she was also curious as to how her eye had healed so quickly.* 'Can you see out of it now?' *she added.*

'Why, yes! I can see out of it just fine, thanks for asking. All has nearly been restored. Soon, all will finally be as it should.'

'What do you mean? What's changed?'

The old woman grinned. 'Why, you've changed, of course. You just haven't realized it yet. And your friend Daniel is undergoing a few changes of his own. As I said, all is nearly as it should be.'

Kasheena felt confusion creeping up into the back of her mind. Only a few moments ago she had felt that the answers to her questions were nearly within her grasp, but now they seemed to be drifting away with the lofting smoke from the fire. She was frustrated and her frustration was quickly turning to anger. She was certain of just one thing: the old woman had deceived her.

'There is no he is there, Grandmother? It's only been you all along, hasn't it? You're the one that sent me into the corridor without a torch to light the way. You're the one that tried to poison me with a pouch of herbs. You're the one that was waiting for me here in the burial ground, not him. What was in the cavern with me, old woman? What did you send to torment me?'

'Why,' *the old woman replied, as though the answer to the question were entirely obvious,* 'Exactly what you'd expect to find in a cavern, I suppose. Bats. Insects. Maybe a lizard or two. And as far as tormenting you goes, you did that to yourself. I couldn't have done half as good a job as you did. Who knows what frightens you better than you do?'

'Are you telling me that I imagined all that?' *She couldn't help* but jump to her feet. 'Are you telling me that there wasn't anything in the cavern except for some dumb old bats and lizards?'

'Imagination's a powerful thing, Child.'

'I...I don't believe you.'

'Did you actually see anything?' the old woman asked, raising an eyebrow. 'Did anything bring you harm? Other than yourself?'

Kasheena's mind raced as she tried to piece together what she had experienced in the cavern. Something had brushed by her in the corridor, of that she was certain. But it had been too dark to see what it was.' It could have been anything,' she admitted to herself. She looked across the fire at the old woman. 'And what about the rustling and scratching noises? Were those just from a bat? And what about the pouch of herbs? Was that my imagination, too? Why would you tie something around my neck that would sting my eyes and nose so badly?'

The old woman looked up at Kasheena with empathy. 'I'm sorry about the herbs, Child, I really am. I knew they would irritate you, but I had to make the batch strong enough to last. I knew you would try to dig your way out of the cavern instead of turning back. The herbs slowed your breathing and heart long enough for you to make it through the dirt, that is all.'

'Why did you put me through such an awful ordeal? I almost died in that horrible place! I almost suffocated!'

'Child, you were never in any real danger.' The old woman poked at the fire with a stick and it flared. 'I could have pulled you from the cavern any time I wanted to. But I had to find out if you were strong enough to make it through on your own. It was all a part of the deal I struck with him. It was to teach you the lesson you needed to learn before you could move forward on your journey.'

'Lesson?' Kasheena asked, shaking her head. 'What lesson are you talking about?'

'Child, think about it for a moment.' The old woman made an impatient gesture. 'You're smart enough to figure it out on your own. What did you learn from your experience in the cavern?'

Kasheena thought long and hard about the question. She tried to visualize her journey through the cavern. She tried to separate the reality of what she had experienced from what she had probably only imagined. The answer came to her slowly, but it came nonetheless, and after a time she looked upon the old woman as if in understanding.

'What did you learn?' The old woman asked for a second time.

'I learned not to trust anyone with a snake painted on their arm,' Kasheena answered with a grin. The old woman burst into laughter and Kasheena giggled and walked over to her and sat down beside her. The two women sat laughing for a time, but their merriment soon subsided. Kasheena took the old woman by the hand and looked her in the eye. 'I think I have learned many things this day, Grandmother, but I believe the most important thing I've learned is that I can be my own worst enemy. I've learned that sometimes the person we should be most frightened of is ourself.'

The old woman looked at Kasheena with satisfaction. 'Yes, Child,' she said in a quiet voice, turning her gaze to the fire, 'that's what you needed to learn. But I'm afraid there's more to it than that.'

'What now, Grandmother? What more do you ask of me? Haven't I endured enough for one day?'

'Many days have passed, but that's not something I can explain to you in a way that you would understand. And it isn't I who ask more of you.' She paused, focusing her vision as if seeking a sign within the flames before them. 'It is he that does the asking now.'

'So what happens now?' Daniel asked, feeling as though he had stuck his foot smack-dab into the middle of a trap the birdman had laid for him.

'Now you will sit with me, Healer. You will stay with me until the morning. Between now and then, I will show you many things.'

'That's it? That's all? All I have to do is sit with you?'

The enormous man smiled down at him, his eyes beginning to glow again. 'You will find, Healer, that sitting with me through the night is much easier spoken than done.'

'Grandmother, what are you staring at? What do you see in the flames?'

'I see him, of course. And I see Daniel, as well.'

'Daniel!' She was excited to hear his name. 'He's here? Is he okay? Can you show him to me? Can I see him?'

The old woman pondered these questions for a moment. 'Yes,' she finally replied. 'I can show him to you, but he is much older than he was when last you saw him. And what you ask comes with a price. If I show you Daniel, you will forever have the Sight, though not nearly as developed as mine. Having the Sight is as much a curse as it is a gift. It carries with it the burden of responsibility. There are other things you must accept responsibility for tonight, other things you must face. And I warn you. If I show you Daniel, you may not like what you see.'

Kasheena accepted the old woman's words with all seriousness. She knew better than to ignore such a warning, but her need to see Daniel again outweighed her concerns. 'I would like to see him,' she whispered. 'I accept the responsibility and consequences of using the Sight.'

Her eyes never leaving the fire, the old woman extended an arm and said, 'Take my hand. Take my hand and prepare yourself for what you are about to see.'

As Kasheena took the old woman's hand the world around them began to change. The old woman's left eye turned pure white. The burial ground slowly faded away. The fire transformed into a ball of bluish-white light. Kasheena felt as though she were rising into the air, and soon a warm wind encircled the two women, then the air around them grew heavy.

'Can you see him, Child? Can you see your friend?'

'No, Grandmother, I can't...I...' She paused. She could almost see something. Vague shapes and figures began to appear all around

her but they were distorted and blurred, like reflections on a pool of rippling water. Kasheena concentrated on the forms and as she did her left eye faded to a dull gray, then changed to a brilliant white. 'Great Spirit!' she cried out as the world around her came into focus. She saw her old friend. She saw who – what - was sitting next to him.

The man was as enormous as he was terrifying to behold. There was a darkness to his presence unlike anything Kasheena had ever seen before. Looking upon him was like staring into an endless void that was somehow staring back at her: He was infinity in the form of a man, a man that could see into her soul and know all her secrets. The birdman had Daniel trapped, enfolded within a pair of monstrously huge hawk's wings. He was screaming.

'What's happening?' Kasheena cried out, horrified by what she was seeing. 'What is he doing to Daniel?'

'Hush, Child. What's happening to your friend is what needs to happen, nothing more, nothing less. And he is only performing his function. He is only fulfilling his end of our bargain.'

'I don't understand! What is this bargain you keep talking about? What does it have to do with me and Daniel?'

'Why, it has everything to do with you and Daniel. You protected Daniel when he was a boy, just like I protected you, and he honored your bravery and my kindness by sparing your lives. But we soon discovered that our actions came with a price. By protecting you and sparing the boy, we changed the natural order of things, and as a result we each lost a part of our Sight and could no longer perform our functions properly. So we made a bargain with each other to set things right and restore the balance. Our actions also created changes in you and the boy that would have affected you adversely later on in your lives. We had to take steps to make that right, too. We had no other choice.'

'Who is he?' Kasheena begged. 'Who are you? Please tell me.'

'We are each an inseparable part of the other. We are the balance within everything that is. My gifts to him are meaning and purpose;

his gifts to me are value and worth. Death has no purpose without life, Child, and life has no value without death.'

'I still don't understand. If you're who I think you are, how is it that you look like real people? How is it that you're flesh and blood?'

'As I have already told you, Child, you see us in forms you can understand, forms your mind can accept. To see us in our true forms, you need look no further than within yourself.'

Kasheena thought she understood. 'You're one of the spirits, aren't you?'

The old woman said nothing.

'And he's a spirit, too, and he's here to take Daniel. Isn't he?'

'No, Child. It's far too late for that. Daniel has never faced things within himself that he must face if he is to become a whole person and a great healer. He's never accepted death. He's never faced his fear of it, and until he does he will be unable to fulfill his true destiny. He is not here to take Daniel. He is only here to show him the things that he must see. I'm afraid it's the only way to set things right again.'

'Take the Sight from me, Grandmother.' Kasheena begged. 'If this is what must happen, I don't want to see it. I can't watch Daniel suffer so much pain.'

'You have to watch. You hold responsibility. You're the one that put Daniel into this situation in the first place. You're responsible for a great many things when it comes to your old friend.'

"Wh - what?' Tears welled in Kasheena's eyes as the truth of the old woman's words dawned in her. She was the one responsible for her friend's predicament. There was no way around it. She began to sob. 'I only wanted to help him. I didn't mean for any of this to happen.'

'I know, Child. I know. You couldn't have known how things would turn out. But I - I should have known better. Don't feel so bad for yourself or your friend. If Daniel is to become a strong man and a great healer, he must endure many painful visions. But he will also be shown wondrous things, things that most people can only dream

of ever seeing. You're responsible for that as well.'

'I don't understand.' Kasheena said, drying her eyes. 'What else am I responsible for?'

'Because of you, Daniel has set off on a quest to learn the ways of healing the spirit. Because of you, he will heal the minds, bodies and spirits of many people from many tribes. Because of you, he will learn to walk between the worlds. He will know a destiny far greater than he would have if the two of you had never met.'

'Can he see me? Does Daniel know I'm here?'

'A part of him can feel your presence but for now it is only a small part. He has yet to learn the ways of the spirit and as I told you when we first met, the place where you dwell is between the worlds, not on one side or the other, but somewhere in the middle. Your friend Daniel is in the world of the living. Like you, he has been infected with the Sight, but it will take both of you a long time to develop it and to learn how to use it properly.'

'How much longer must Daniel endure the visions? How much longer will he suffer?'

The old woman sighed. 'They will subside, Child. But like any true seeker of the spirit, he will endure the visions for the rest of his life. Like any true healer, he will suffer for as long as others are in pain.'

Kasheena was about to ask the old woman if Daniel were destined to become shaman when, without warning, a tremendous gust of wind blew by her and a flash of blindingly bright light lit up the burial ground. In an instant the birdman was gone. Daniel was lying on the ground, shaking as though he were freezing.

'Now that's interesting,' the old woman quipped. 'That's quite interesting indeed.'

'What is it, Grandmother? What happened?'

'It didn't take nearly as long as I expected it would. Your friend is strong, stronger than I gave him credit for. But he's endured a lot in a very short time. I must go now. I must take my leave of you and go to Daniel. He'll be needing me, I expect.'

'Can I go to him?'

'No, Child, you cannot.'

'How do I find my way out of this place? How will I find my way back home?'

The old woman let go of Kasheena's hand and as her touch ended, the world around her began to change. The ball of bluish-white light grew dim, and Kasheena could feel herself drifting away from the old woman, away from her friend Daniel.

'Grandmother! Will I ever see you again?' she called as the old woman's form faded away.

'If you look hard enough, you will see me many times in many things. Seek me in your spirit, Child,' her voice was almost as indistinct as her form. 'Seek me in your heart...' And with those words, the old woman was gone.

The faded ball of light began to glow with hues of orange and red. The light grew brighter and soon Kasheena was bathed in flickering firelight. She sat silent and still in the burial ground, overcome with a profound sadness. The old woman had been hard on her, tougher than anyone had ever been, but now that she was gone, Kasheena felt empty and alone.

The old woman would probably have scolded her for feeling sorry for herself. She would have told her to be happy for the time they had together. She would have reassured her that she would get along just fine on her own. The old woman had tried her patience and tested her convictions. She had put her through the most harrowing experience of her life, but Kasheena was a stronger and wiser person for having known her. She noticed that the turtle shell was lying on the ground next to her. Thinking about Daniel and everything they had been through, she picked it up and slowly turned it in her hands. The fire snapped, sending sparks into the air and breaking her out of her malaise. When she looked up, what she saw across the fire from her caused her heart to pound in her chest like a drum. She had no idea how long the birdman had been sitting there watching her and that thought alone sent a chill washing over her. Her every instinct urged her to run but she sat motionless and stared into the man's black eyes.

'Where is the old woman?'

Kasheena said nothing.

'She is with him already, then? I didn't think it would take very long. Tell me, did she reveal to you why I chose to appear in the form of a hawk?'

Kasheena just stared at him.

He nodded as if she had replied. 'Certainly someone from your tribe has spoken to you of the hawk spirit, haven't they? What does the hawk symbolize to your tribe?'

'Messenger,' Kasheena answered in a faint whisper.

'I didn't quite hear you. Could you say that again?'

Kasheena's eyes narrowed. 'I said messenger!' Her hatred of the birdman overcame her fear of him.

'You need not fear me,' he said easily. 'Your hatred of me is misplaced. To you, I am a symbol of something you despise, something unspeakable. But to the old and the sick,' he touched his chest, 'to those who no longer have purpose, I am the herald of rest and clemency. I am the blessed kiss of the Great Spirit itself. It is true that I am sometimes called upon to deliver those who are young and full of life, but that is the way of things. I hold no dominion over the way. I am only a messenger, a simple doorman. I am a watcher between your world and that of the ancestors and spirits.'

Kasheena made no reply.

The man rose to his feet. 'Young one,' he said from his full height, 'It is obvious you are not ready to speak with me. I will be on my way. When you are ready, return to where you entered into the burial ground and I will come to you. At that time, you will have a choice to make.'

At that moment, Kasheena noticed that the man was holding something in his hands, something familiar. It was the shaman's staff!

'Wait,' she almost shouted, rising to her feet as well. 'Where did you get that staff? That doesn't belong to you. It doesn't belong to me, either. That staff belongs to my tribe's shaman. I want it back.'

'Why, certainly.' He extended it to her. 'It was broken when I took it but it has been restored. You are welcome to take the staff from me anytime you wish. But before it will do you any good, you must make a choice.'

'What choice?' she asked, still frightened but certain she would have to hear him out before he gave her the staff.

'Your destination. The staff will carry you to the next leg of your journey. But until you have chosen a destination, it is all but worthless to you.'

'I don't understand,' she said. 'So far I haven't been given any choice as to where to go. I'm still not even sure where I am.'

'The old woman didn't explain this to you? She didn't tell you where you are?'

'She told me that this place is between the worlds, but that's all that she said. She didn't tell me how to leave or even what I'm supposed to do next.'

'I see...' The birdman turned his gaze to the fire, pondering what to say next. After a few moments, a hint of a smile came to his face. He sat down again.

'Sit with me,' he said. 'Sit with me, and I will show you many things.'

Kasheena's heart began to pound. The birdman terrified her but she knew she dared not show any fear. 'I saw what you did to Daniel,' she replied in an icy voice. 'I saw the horrors you put him through and if you think I'm going to allow you to do the same to me without a fight you're wrong.'

The birdman smiled up at her, but not in a way that was comforting. 'I have already told you that you have nothing to fear from me. You have already faced me down and that is rare indeed. Most won't even acknowledge my existence. But not you. You faced me without the slightest hesitation. You are brave without question, one of the bravest mortals I have ever met.' He smiled again. 'But *now that you are back in my presence, you are second-guessing yourself. If you question your bravery now, it will slowly begin trickling away until there is none left inside you.'*

Still refusing to sit down, Kasheena considered his words. She didn't trust him but in some inexplicable way what he said made sense. She had been second-guessing herself. She had allowed her fear of him to chisel away at her courage. But the old woman was gone now and had given no indication that she would return. The only way out of the burial grounds, Kasheena realized, was to go through him.

'What is it you expect of me?' she demanded.

'Only what you would expect of yourself.'

Kasheena drew in a deep breath. A light drizzle began to fall in the burial ground She exhaled. 'I would expect myself to be brave.' She walked around the fire and sat down next to him

Daniel opened his eyes to the blaze of morning sun but his mind was still clouded by the visions of the night before.'Was it all just a dream?' he asked himself. Had the birdman been real? Or had he been a hallucination? The birdman had shown him many things, things both terrible and beautiful to behold. He had seen the darkness in the heart of humanity and the brilliant light of untainted spirit. He had seen his worst fears becoming reality, his greatest hopes being fulfilled. He was coming to realize that it didn't matter if it had only been a dream or a hallucination. It didn't matter if the birdman had been real or a phantom. The impact of the visions would have been the same and Daniel knew that he had seen more in a single night than he had during his entire lifetime.

A shadow suddenly blocked out the sun. As he looked up, he saw an old woman with a kindly face and dark skin looking down at him. His vision was still hazy and as he squinted and tried to get a clearer focus, he saw that it wasn't an old woman at all. It was the shaman.

The shaman looked at him with concern. 'You do not look well, my friend,' he remarked as he wrapped Daniel in a blanket and laid one hand on the side of his face. 'The spirits must have shown you many unwelcome things.'

A dragonfly buzzed around Daniel's head, then came to rest on the shaman's shoulder. Daniel looked up at the shaman and smiled.

Kasheena's gaze searched the burial ground, still trying to make sense of what was happening. So much of what she was seeing she didn't understand. Many of the symbols and totems were unfamiliar to her. She wondered at their significance.

'I understand that it is confusing to you.' the birdman remarked, as though he had been reading her mind.

'It's just that I don't recognize most of the markings,' she replied, still looking at the graves and altars.

'No...I don't suppose you would. The altars and the signs on them are symbolic of those who have passed through the gateway to the overworld. They are merely echoes, reflections of other times and other places. They are the imprinted memories of lives spent in the middle world.'

'So they're memorials to honor the ancestors?'

'Yes.' The birdman's left eye faded from black to gray. 'But many are monuments of tribes you have never seen before,' he continued. 'Many are the symbols of civilizations far removed from your own. Look at them. Look at those who have passed through my gateway. Look at the Great Ancestors. Through them, you will see your next destination.'

His left eye turned brilliant white and as it did, Kasheena's left eye began to fade as well. Suddenly, she was seeing apparitions; the ghostly forms of the ancestors moving through the burial ground, and on to the overworld. Some of their skins were colors she had never seen before. Some were dressed in ceremonial clothing that was unfamiliar but beautiful just the same. Looking upon the ancestors filled her with a peace she had never felt before. She had thought about her own ancestors many times in the past, and each time she *did, it had filled her with a great sadness. She had always viewed death as an ending, the finality from which there was no return. Now, looking upon the spirits of the Great Ancestors, she realized that death was not closure. It was the beginning of a new adventure. Maybe the spirits of the ancestors were having journeys like hers, wondrous new adventures.*

'I think I understand now,' she said to the birdman. 'I think I finally realize who and what you are.' 'Then no longer will you look upon me with fear,' he said as a huge pair of pure white wings rose into the air above him. 'No longer will you think of me with despair in your heart.'

A single feather fell from each wing, slowing spiraling down, finally coming to rest on Kasheena's lap. She instinctively reached for the feathers, and as she took them into her hands, she gasped at what she was seeing.

'The spirits have offered me two wonderful destinations from which to choose! They have seen what is in my heart. They have blessed me with two fantastic opportunities.'

'Yes,' the birdman agreed. 'But either choice comes with a price. Choices always do. This is the way of making choices. There is no way around it.'

'Yes. It is a most difficult decision.'

'Take your time, young one. I will stay with you for as long as you need me. As you have already learned, it is best to think things out before acting.'

'No,' she said in a near whisper. 'I mean, I already know what I have to do. In some ways, the decision is one I made a very long time ago. To change my mind now would be to betray my own heart.'

'I understand,' he replied. 'What is it to be?'

Kasheena looked at the feather in her right hand. This feather would allow her to travel to the village of the Great Ancestors, where she could stay with them for a time and learn the secrets of the spirit. She looked at the feather in her left hand. This feather would allow her to return home to her village, to the ones she loved most.

'How do I make it work?' she asked.'"Give me the feather you have chosen and I will help you on your way.'

Kasheena offered him the feather of her choosing and he fastened it to the top of the shaman's staff. He took the second feather from her hand, and he wove it into a braid in her hair.

'That one is for protection on your journey,' he said with a smile. 'Few are those that would dare trifle with my medicine.'

Lastly, the birdman handed her the shaman's staff. 'It is time. The decision has been made. There is no turning back. Do not forget to take the spirit-shell with you. It has become a symbol of your medicine, and you have earned the right to bear it many times over.'

'Spirit-shell?' She looked bewildered. Then, 'Oh, yes. I understand!' She bent down and retrieved the turtle shell from the ground. She had no sooner done so, when the shaman's staff began to gently vibrate in her hand, then it started to glow with an ethereal light. A strong wind began to blow, and the world around her began to change. She began to rise into the air. The ground below her whirled and churned. A portal to the destination she had chosen opened.

'I had nearly forgotten!' the birdman shouted so he could be heard over the high-pitched whistling of the winds. 'The old woman asked me to give this to you. She said you would be needing it."

He reached up to her and handed her a small, smooth stone. Kasheena recognized it. It was the stone she had found in Daniel's dream world. She rolled it in her palm, glad to have it back. One side of the stone had been carved with a glyph of a turtle. The other side was now carved with a glyph of a snake.

Her hair whipping madly in the powerful winds, she looked down at the birdman. A dragonfly buzzed by her head, then flew down and came to rest on his shoulder. He began to fade away, and just before he vanished completely, she thought she heard him speak a single word.

Dreamwalker.

Kasheena disappeared into the village far below.

The Medicine Symbols

As you continue your shamanic travels, you should now be on the lookout for things that are symbolic of your spiritual journey. We will refer to these things as your *medicine symbols*. For example, thus far in her story, Kasheena has collected (or been given) certain items that she believes to be important aids in her quest to become shaman. The turtle shell, the healing stone, the shaman's staff, even the hawk feathers are symbolic of things she hopes to accomplish, or hurdles she has overcome.

The medicine symbols I chose for Kasheena represent animal spirits but your own medicine symbols might be very different. For example, if nature and flourishing life are meaningful to you spiritually and you were to come across a species of life (animal or plant) that reminds you of all things that grow, you might want to consider choosing it as one of your medicine symbols. This can be anything from seaweed to a mighty oak or from your domestic cat to an African elephant.

Your medicine symbols can be anything that you can hear, see, smell, taste or touch. If sunlight reminds you of your own inner light, then you can consider using the sun as a symbol of your medicine. If water reminds you of the depth and flow of your spirit, you could use water as a symbol of your medicine. What about the hoot of an owl or the screech of a hawk? What about the scent of lavender or ocean salt? Even your own heart could be a powerful symbol of your medicine.

As you go about the task of choosing the medicine symbols that are right for you, keep in mind that the true power isn't in the symbol, or even in what the symbol represents. The medicine symbols are only *reminders* of the things you hold important and that are spiritually meaningful to you and your spiritual journey. They are symbolic of the things you have learned, or perhaps the things that you need to learn. They are symbolic of the things that inspire you to create. They are mere symbols of a greater power; the power of your own healing spirit.

Medicine cannot heal until the healer has properly administered it.

Tending the Fires Goal Three:

Seeking the Spirit of the Wolf

That very night in Max's room a forest grew. And grew-
and grew until the ceiling hung with vines and the
walls became the world all around.
Maurice Sendak, *Where the Wild Things Are*

In the last leg of your shamanic travels you entered into the
lower world where you laid claim to the second (or inner)
medicine wheel and caught your first glimpse of the Great
Tribe. You began working with some of the animal spirits that
inhabit the lower world as well. On the next leg of your
journey, you will return to the lower world, where you will
become acquainted with the members of the Great Tribe and
gain insight into their spiritual practices. You will also be
seeking out a companion to accompany you on your spiritual
journey. We go now to meet this new companion. Let us set
off in search of the Great Wolf Spirit.

The Call of the Wild
Depending on which authors work you read or web site you
peruse, the wolf (or wolf spirit/totem) can symbolize many
different things and hold many different meanings. There is,
however, a common thread that runs through many of the
writings of those who have worked with wolves or the wolf
spirit: the wolf represents all that is wild and free. In her
book, *Women Who Run With the Wolves, Myths and Stories of the
Wild Woman Archetype,*[12] author Clarissa Pinkola Estés states
that all of us, especially women, possess a wild-instinctual
nature that can be reclaimed if it is desired strongly enough.

The spirit of the wolf is all about this wild nature. The wolf instinctively knows how to survive, how to hunt, how to correctly choose a mate and how to care for the pack. The wolf is wild and free, and can teach us many valuable lessons about our own instincts and spiritual needs. The wolf is thus the perfect companion to accompany (or help guide) you on your shamanic travels.

While considering the benefits of companionship with the wolf spirit, I was once again inspired by the work of my good friend, author Carol Rosinski. I was delighted when Carol mailed me a letter detailing her early experiences of working with the wolves. What follows is a brief description of these early workings in Carol's own words.

'At first, a wolf would meet me on the edge of my dreams, and we would run through meadows, forest and the stars until I lost him and I'd fall asleep. Again and again, we would run and I would be left behind. Even though it was happening at bedtime while I was lying down, it was exhausting! Finally, I started

to understand that he was teaching me to hunt by acting as the prey. So I learned to "hunt" him by smell, by hearing, and by other senses that I had never used in that way.

That was before my first full trance. My first full trance happened soon after I quit my job and started writing and drawing full time again. I was sitting at the back of our property, at the edge of a wood, and I had the impression that a wolf was standing in front of me. I gave myself over to the notion that a different reality existed right beside this one, and that I could see into it if I wanted to. The sensation of this black wolf was so strong that I'll always remember it. I could see his eyes, smell his fur and his breath, and feel the heat off his body. It was a very fulfilling experience for me. The wolf then ran off into the woods, just like he had been doing all along. I followed (in my trance state) and he led me to what I needed to see and understand at that moment.

Wolves are all about trust and devotion. I give my full trust to *my wolf guides, and I know that trust is protected and safe. I know my wolves won't lead me where I want to go; they'll lead me where I need to be. I don't have that level of trust with many. Animals are different than people. You can trust them to not have an agenda.*

So many "wolvy" things have happened to me since you last asked about my work. Wolf charities have been sending me email and snail-mail and now I see a brochure with a wolf on it I picked up months ago has resurfaced here at my computer desk. One of the biggest lessons that I have learned from the Wolf is not to chew on a bone with no meat on it. I tend to occasionally pick out lovely "bones" and chew and chew and chew them ... and get little or nothing in return. I'm thinking about meaty things now. Things I can do that really nourish me. So thank you for reminding me of my wolves. I think I need to listen to them intently for a while.'[13]

Reading Carol's letter, I was struck by her observation of how the wolves had "coincidentally" resurfaced in her life because I had asked her to account her personal experiences of working with them. I was also struck by her admission of needing to recount the lessons of her wolves' teachings. I was intrigued by the possibility that the things that were once spiritually meaningful to us, but that we have forgotten, never really leave us. Perhaps they are always around us, and we have simply suppressed them to the point of no longer noticing them. Perhaps they still lurk in the shadowy places in our spirits and our minds, and resurface from time to time with fresh lessons when we are in need of their council.

The Spirit of the Wolf

If you attempted to make contact with the animal spirits during your first descent into the lower world, it is possible that you have already met wolf. If so, upon returning to the lower world, you should further this contact and express to wolf your desire for him or her to accompany you on your spiritual journey. Keep in mind, however, that it may take time for a wolf to fully accept you and agree to become your spiritual companion. Wolf may have its own ideas and opinions of the things you need to learn. For me personally, I found it necessary to work with wolf for a time outside the middle world before he agreed to accompany me on my shamanic travels. I did this work in meditation. As you may also find it necessary to first work with wolf by using a similar technique, I will now share with you the meditation that I used to make first contact with my wolf companion.

It was the middle of January when I first began meditating on the wolf spirit. Where I live, temperatures in January are well below freezing. Although I felt that the best place to meditate on the wolf spirit would be in the great outdoors, I knew I would freeze if I sat out in the cold of a January night. Through meditation I developed a way to bring the great outdoors to the great indoors. The perfect indoor location to meditate on the wolf spirit was in my shamanic room, although at first I found it a bit difficult to restrain myself from entering into a shamanic state and trekking off for the spirit lands.

Before undertaking the meditation, it is useful to prepare an offering to entice the wolf spirit to approach you. Living wild wolves thrive on nourishment, and the wolf *spirit* is no different. The offering you make should therefore provide the wolf spirit with sustenance in one form or another. Preparing an offering for the wolf spirit is relatively easy to do, and only requires a bit of forethought and preparation. The easiest way to prepare an offering for the wolf spirit is to create what I refer to as a *totem candle*. To create your own totem candle, you will need to acquire an everyday household candle and "charge" it with nourishing energies. To do this charging, hold the candle in your hands and concentrate your thoughts on things that the wolf spirit would find fulfilling. The wolf spirit is the vital essence of all things wild and free, so concentrate on the wild nature of your own spirit and visualize this energy entering into the candle's wick. The wolf spirit thrives on the love and companionship of the pack, so find these same qualities within yourself and use them to charge the candle as well. The wolf spirit will be attracted by the energies of the totem candle as well as being "nourished" by them.

Note: The Meditation of the Wolf Spirit may not work for you "off the shelf." You may find it necessary to tailor the meditation to your own personal needs, taste, or situation.

The Meditation of the Wolf Spirit

Dim the lights in your room, and find a comfortable place to sit. Relax your body and your mind. Light the wick of the totem candle and speak aloud this invocation:

I call upon the spirit of nature, of all things wild and free.
I call upon the spirit of wolf, and bid him be known to me.
Through plains and forests of the night, with wolf I am free to
    run.
To the wild pack my heart and spirit belong, until our journey is
    done.

Look around the room and observe the play of dancing shadows and flickering candlelight. Know that pack is with you, concealed within the shadows, silently watching and waiting. Close your eyes and open yourself to the spirit of the wolf.

You visualize the room in which you now sit, every corner and every crevice. You concentrate until you can see the room clearly in your mind.

Slowly, everything around you starts to change. The walls of the room begin to fade away, as though becoming transparent. Just beyond the walls, you see the vague outlines of distant trees and branches, gently swaying in a warm, evening breeze. You feel the soft touch of this breeze as it blows across your skin. The floor begins to change as well. It becomes craggy and you soon see that wild woodland grasses are somehow sprouting from the floor and growing all around you. Everything in the room seems to be coming to life. Vines, bushes and trees take root and shoot up from the ground. Plant life is now growing over every surface in the room. Soon, the last traces of the room disappear altogether as they give way to this thick growth. You are now sitting in the center of a wild and ancient forest.

You look up and you see starlight twinkling in the night sky through breaks in the lofty clouds. You smell the thick, musky scent of loam and moss, of trees as old as time. You hear the distant calls of nocturnal birds and animals echoing from deep within the forest. A mist begins to flow from somewhere beyond the shadowy tree line and it slowly moves over the ground in fingerlike wisps of vapor. Suddenly, you sense a presence. You know that you are not alone.

You look deep into the forest. A pair of shiny-yellow eyes are looking back at you from the shadows. You hear a soft, yet rapid panting sound. You know that you are in the presence of the wolf. His company makes you feel wild and free.

You call out to the wolf and he takes several steps out of darkness and toward you. His fur gleams with a brilliant gloss in the starlight. There is a twinkle of eagerness in his eyes. Then, without warning, he turns from you and bolts into the forest. You instinctively know that you are to follow. You spring to your feet and follow him into the shadows.

As you go more deeply into the forest, your senses become keener. Your spirit grows wilder and you begin to feel a oneness with everything around you. You are more in tune with the natural world than you have ever been before. You start to run.

Even though the forest is dark, you have no fear of it. You can see and hear everything. You can *feel* everything. You sense that the wolf is just ahead of you, and you quicken your pace. Your heart beats in your chest like a tribal drum. Your blood runs hot through your veins and you are growing wilder and wilder as you run. You feel long-forgotten instincts sharpening within you. You smell a thousand scents on the night air and you know what each of them is. You run faster and faster. You are almost upon the wolf now, almost one with him. You look down at your feet but they are no longer there. Instead, you see swift and sure paws rocketing you through the night forest. You have become one with the wolf, and you truly know what it means to be wild and free.

Your breath grows thin and you slow your pace. You breathe deeply of the night air and it feels cool and welcome in your chest. You feel satisfied by the untamed run, satisfied with yourself. You feel yourself slowly rising up, away from the wolf. You feel yourself returning to your own body.

Suddenly, you are seeing through your own eyes. You feel the beating of your own heart. You have returned to where you met the wolf and began your run. You are sitting in the center of a wild and ancient forest and now, slowly, everything around you begins to change. The forest begins to fade away, as though becoming transparent. Just beyond the diminishing tree line, you see the vague outlines of your room. The trees and plant life begin to recede as though returning to the seeds from which they came. The wild woodland grasses recede and as you look down you see the floor of your room. The forest is gone, and you have returned home.

You open your eyes to your earthly reality. The spirit of the wolf is still in your heart.

I hope that you enjoyed The Spirit of the Wolf Meditation as much as I did undertaking it and writing it out for you. I also hope that it will assist you on your spiritual journey. Now that you have been introduced to your wolf guide in meditation, it is time to return to the middle world where you will meet wolf in his/her own territory. You will also walk the spoke of the medicine wheel and enter the land of the Great Tribe.

Shamanic Traveling Path Three:
The Great Tribe

The goal of your third journey into the spirit lands is threefold:

One - to choose your first medicine symbol.

Two - to descend to the lower world and begin working with the wolf spirit in its own territory.

Three - to walk the spoke of the inner medicine wheel and enter into the land of the Great Tribe. Once you have entered this land, you will spend time becoming acquainted with the tribal members and familiarizing yourself with their spiritual practices.

The preparation and technique for your third adventure in shamanic traveling will be the same as they were on your previous travels. Before you undertake the third journey, however, you should spend some time meditating on the three goals I laid out for you. The time has come for you to enhance your spiritual journeying by devising and incorporating some of your own techniques into your travels. This isn't to say that you should deviate from achieving the goals that I have set forth for you, only that you should now be thinking about ways in which you can add to the process to make it more meaningful to you on a spiritual level. For example, you can meditate on how you yourself find meaning and beauty in your day-to-day life and seek out your first medicine symbol in the same way. As I stated at the beginning of this book, *Neither I nor any other teacher can simply take a person by the hand and lead them into spirituality. I cannot pull it out of my pocket and present it to them as a gift.* I cannot tell you what spirituality is or what it means to be spiritual. I cannot tell you where to find it. These are questions that only you can answer. These are things that only you can discover. By taking you on this journey, the best that I can do is to guide you to new places to explore where you can make your own spiritual discoveries. The best that I can hope for is that by sharing a bit of my magic with you, that your own magic will be enhanced by the experience. Only you can answer the question of what the Great Spirit is and what it means to you. Seek it out and share what you find with the rest of us.

By now you should have a pretty good handle on shamanic traveling, so I will dispense with refreshing your memory. Just make sure that you have carefully thought out the goals of the third journey before you decide to undertake it. Your third journey shouldn't be rushed and you may find it necessary to return to the spirit lands and the lower world several times to accomplish your objectives. Beyond the three goals that I have set-forth, your third journey will be free-form and you will be relying on your own spirit to guide you. You already know the way to the spirit lands and how to descend to the lower world. You know how to contact the animal spirits and find the spoke of the medicine wheel that leads to the Great Tribe. All that's left to discuss is your pending visit with the Great Tribe.

I have already provided you with a graphic description of how to open up a pathway that leads to the Great Tribe but if you need refreshing you should go back and re-read the visualization on page 54 of this book. Once you've opened the pathway, it's a simple matter of walking it until it leads you to the land of the Great Tribe. Once you have arrived in the tribal land, it is important to note the location of the pathway so you don't get lost trying to find it when it's time to return home. As I have already explained, the Great Tribe will accept you unconditionally, so you shouldn't be fearful of being rejected or turned away. Just remember to treat the members of the tribe as you would expect them to treat you.

Your first order of business is to become acquainted with the tribal members; secondly, to familiarize yourself with the tribe's spiritual practices. During the fourth (and final) journey you will accompany the Great Tribe as they make a spiritual migration. It's important, therefore, to spend as much time with the tribe as necessary to build a strong bond with them. When you're ready to return home, simply return to the pathway and follow it back to the lower world. From there you will ascend to the spirit lands and follow the path that leads home. As you undertake this next journey, keep in mind that you can accomplish the three goals in any order you desire. You can make as many return trips to the lower world and the Great Tribe as you need to make.

The way is set, so I will detain you no further. Go now, and seek the spirit of the wolf. Seek him in the lower world, seek him within yourself. Walk the spoke of the medicine wheel, enter the land of the Great Tribe. Tend the embers, build the fire of the Great Spirit within. I will be waiting for you when you return.

Emergence Part Four:

The Three

"You know that place between asleep and awake, the place
where you can still remember dreaming? That's where I'll
always love you...that's where I'll be waiting."
– Peter Pan

*Kasheena lay quietly in her bed, wondering at her dreams. Dreaming
in the ancestral village wasn't the same as dreaming had been back
home. Sleeping wasn't the same, either, and she was having a hard
time figuring out why everything was so different. Here, her dreams
were more like lessons than the fancies of her imagination. In the
past, her dreams had been filled with the people she loved and cared
about most but now she only dreamed of the ancestors who would
alight in the village and then depart almost as quickly as they had
arrived. She understood why many of the new arrivals left so
quickly. The Three had explained that much, at least. What she
didn't understand was why she was dreaming of these ancestors.
Every night she fell asleep, and every night one of the ancestors came
to her in her dreams to teach her something new.*

*Every night, that is, until last night. In last night's dream, she
had climbed to the top of the mountain that overlooked the ancestral
village in search of the Great Spirit. The Three had told her that the
Great Spirit dwells in the mountain, and that if she were patient,
one day she would be allowed to climb the mountain and the Great
Spirit would teach her a lesson. This would be the last lesson she
needed to learn before she left the ancestral village.*

*She had no idea how long she'd been with the Great Ancestors.
Time was different here. It felt like many years had passed. She felt
like she'd grown up. She pulled back the covers and let out a mighty*

yawn. She would go to The Three and speak with them of her dream.

Daniel packed the last of his belongings in a duffle bag and looked around his apartment. The emptiness of the room was both comforting and disturbing. The absoluteness of his decision hung over him like a ghost that only he could perceive. He was confident that answering the shaman's summons was the right decision, but he knew that if he left now he would never see his home again. He had returned to the city to sell his possessions and raise as much money as he could to buy medicine. He had called in a few markers as well. Many of the people whose lives he had saved were well to do and he wasn't the least bit shy about asking them for money. Some of them had more coin than they could spend in ten lifetimes. He'd had quite few doors closed in his face, but he had been able to rally enough people to his cause to stockpile a decent supply of medicine. Where he was going, he would be in need of it.

Daniel had spent the last fifteen years of his life traveling from tribe to tribe, learning the ways of healing the spirit. He had honed his medical skills during that time as well. In every tribe he visited, he healed as many of the sick as he could. The shamans of the tribes repaid his kindness by teaching him everything they knew about the spirit medicine. He had thus become so proficient and caring in his work that the tribes had come to call him Great Healer. There was only one village in the tribal lands that he'd never visited. Of all the shamans, there was only one that he had yet to meet. This unknown shaman was said to be a powerful and mysterious old man who lived at the top of the eastern mountain, where he communed with the Great Spirit. Word had spread throughout the tribal lands that the shaman had called for Daniel to come to him to discuss a matter of great importance. Over the years, Daniel had developed a keen intuition, and upon occasion, could see things before they happened. The tribal wise women told him he had the sight. He was pretty sure, therefore, that he already knew what the old shaman wanted to discuss with him, and so he had made the decision to go home and buy medicine and finalize his old life. Tonight, Daniel would set sail *for the tribal lands where he would climb the mountain and go to the shaman.*

The Three were easy enough to find. They usually were. Of all the Great Ancestors, they were the only constant in the village. They were always on hand to give counsel. One was said to have been a great chieftain who had lost his life defending his people. He was a quiet and distant man, but when he spoke there was always wisdom in his words, and he had told Kasheena that she reminded him of his daughter. The second was a beautiful woman with a noble look about her and symbols painted on her face. She carried parchment scrolls that she called her book of stories. It was said that, many years before Kasheena's birth, she had ruled as the matriarch of a great tribe. The third, whose face was always veiled in shadow and whose back was always turned, was said to have been a great shaman who had healed countless people from countless tribes. Whenever Kasheena was in this shaman's presence, she felt protected and strengthened. Of The Three, he was her favorite.

'Great Ancestors.' She greeted with her customary bow. 'I've come to tell you of my dreams. I'm in need of your counsel again.'

'There is no need to bow here,' the matriarch said as she always did. 'In this village we are all equals, and none are greater than any other. Bowing is of another time and place. We can see what is in your heart.'

The chieftain gave Kasheena a nod. The Third was silent.

'I dreamed about the mountain and the Great Spirit,' she told them. 'I dreamed that I climbed to the top of the mountain and learned the final lesson.'

'Then no longer are you in need of our counsel,' the shaman said without hesitation. As usual, his back was turned to her. 'It is clear what must be done.'

'He's right,' the chieftain agreed. 'Do you understand what the dream meant?'

'I...I think so. You've already told me all about the mountain and the great lesson. I haven't forgotten. Does the dream mean it's time

for me to leave?'

'Yes,' the matriarch answered. 'You have stayed with us for a very long time. You have taught as much as you have learned.'

The chieftain nodded again. 'You've reminded us what it was like to be alive,' he said. 'But I suppose there's no delaying the inevitable.' He rose to his feet and extended his hand. 'Come. I will walk with you to the mountain.'

As Kasheena thought about the chieftain's offer, she looked longingly at the shaman. The chieftain looked from one to the other. He understood.

'I will take her as far as the foothills,' the shaman said without turning. 'To the foothills, but no further.'

The chieftain opened his arms and gestured for Kasheena to come to him. She ran to him without hesitation and wrapped her arms around him in a tremendous hug.

'Stuffy, isn't he?' the chieftain whispered in her ear, a wide grin coming over his face. She gave the chieftain a kiss on the cheek and turned her attention to the matriarch.

'I still feel as though I should be bowing to you.' She looked down at her feet.

'If you insist on bowing,' the matriarch said, 'Then I insist on doing the same.' And the two women bowed to each other. If not for the differences in their clothing, it would have been nearly impossible to tell them apart.

Without a word, the shaman began walking toward the mountain. Following after him, Kasheena turned to look at the Great Ancestors one last time. Just for a moment, she thought she saw a snake wrapped around the matriarch's arm and the emblem of a hawk pinned to breast of the chieftain's coat.

As Daniel sailed for the tribal lands, he thought about his life and everything he had experienced. His life had been an amazing journey and he felt blessed by the spirits for all the wonderful things he had seen and done. But at times like tonight, the past came back to haunt him. His ability to heal the sick was as much a blessing as it was a curse. He had saved countless lives over the years, but there had been many beyond his ability to cure. Too many, he thought, and of all the patients he had lost, it was the children that bothered him most. Thinking of the lost children filled his spirit with a great sadness but it strengthened his resolve as well. Each loss had driven him to develop his skills and become a stronger healer. Each loss had been a stepping-stone to greater understanding. The medicine stowed in the belly of the ship was inadequate but it would have to do for now. Although he had learned a great deal about the medicinal properties of the herbs and plants that grew in the tribal lands, there was still a lot of work and research to be done. With the help of the tribal wise women he was well on his way to being able to synthesize his own medicine, and, in time, he was confident that he would have powerful new remedies at his disposal. But that time was still a long way off and it was a five-day sail just to reach the tribal lands. For now he would sleep.

As they walked along, Kasheena thought about her days in the ancestral village and everyone she had met on her life's journey. She thought about her grandmother and her parents, who had died when she was just a little girl. She thought about Daniel. What, she wondered, had become of him?

The foothills were close now, and the shaman hadn't spoken a single word since they'd set off together. She knew their time was drawing to an end. Before the shaman left her there was something she simply had to know.

She summoned up her nerve and spoke. 'Why do you always turn your back to me? Why won't you let me see your face? Don't you like me?'

The shaman stopped walking. He stood in silence for a long time. 'When I was alive,' he finally began,' My people believed that a person's back was symbolic of the strength and support they brought to the tribe. They believed that by intentionally turning their back to someone, they were asking them to remember things that had taken place in the past.'

Kasheena thought about this. 'So by turning your back , you're asking me to remember the past? Is that what you're saying?'

The shaman said nothing. Kasheena was confused and for a moment she thought about pressing the issue. Thinking better of it, she asked, 'What will I learn at the top of the mountain? What does the Great Spirit have in store for me?'

'I can answer neither of those questions,' the shaman said. He began walking again. 'But I can tell you what to look for.

'At the top of the mountain,' he continued, 'is a reflecting pool. On three sides of it are three stones of the same size, but of different shape and color. It is known to me that when you look into the pool you will see the face of the Great Spirit and learn a lesson of considerable importance. Once this lesson is learned, you will leave ancestral lands and begin the next leg of your life's journey.'

Kasheena knew better than to ask any more questions and as they walked toward the mountain she wondered what lesson the Great Spirit might teach her. She thought about the reflecting pool and what she might see on its surface.

Before she knew it, they had reached the foothills. The shaman turned as if to leave.

'Aren't you even going to say goodbye?' she asked him.

For the first time, the shaman turned to her, but his face was still veiled in shadow.

'There is no need to say goodbye to you,' he said. 'When you're ready, you will see me once again. You asked me a question earlier that I didn't honor with an answer. I will answer you now. I hide my face from you because you would find it frightening. Before you can look upon my face, you must first learn to see your own face. You are not yet ready to see the larger truth of your own nature. You are not ready to accept the burden of the future you have chosen for yourself.' And with those words, the shaman turned away and started walking back to the village of the Great Ancestors.

Kasheena watched him until his form was small on the horizon. He had told her many curious things and had left her with many unanswered questions. She turned and looked at the peaks high above her. She had a feeling that she would find the answers at the top of the mountain. She entered the foothills and began her ascent.

As the ship was preparing to dock, Daniel gathered his meager belongings and went below deck to oversee the unloading of his medicine. The trip to the tribal lands had been uneventful and not a single bottle of the medicine had been damaged. It would be a shame to lose anything now. He watched nervously as the crates were hoisted above deck and one by one brought to rest on the pier, which was, more or less, a simple landing that had been built by the handful of natives that lived along the shoreline. Not the grand wharf of a shipyard or harbor town, it was old and in disrepair. The heart of the tribal lands was another two days' journey inland, and the medicine would have to be carted over rough terrain. It still wasn't secure, and until it was he wouldn't be able to relax.

'Welcome home, my friend!'

Hearing a voice, Daniel turned with a wide smile to greet the shaman.

It was good to see the shaman again, and looking at him filled Daniel's mind with old memories. The shaman had been his first teacher. He recalled with clarity the night he had been led to the tribal burial ground, the night he had faced the darkness of his own spirit.

'How have you been?' Daniel called back as he walked over to greet his old friend.

'I've been well, but I'm afraid there isn't any time for pleasantries. I've spoken to the old shaman of the mountain. He sent me to find you. You must go to him immediately. The elders of the western tribe told me that you had traveled to your home for medicine. I've been waiting here for you to return. You must go to the old shaman. You must climb the mountain and hear what he has to say.'

Daniel looked at the crates of medicine, and then at the mountain looming in the east.

The shaman pointed to the crates of medicine. 'There isn't any time for that,' he said. 'I understand that the medicine is of great importance to you but for now you must trust it to my care. I'll summon help and deliver it safely to my village. The old shaman told me that the future of the tribes hinges on your getting to him quickly.'

'I understand,' Daniel said in a quiet voice. 'And I trust you with my life. But I need to ask a favor of you, old friend. I need you to take the medicine to the village in the north, the village in the valley of the butte.'

The shaman nodded. 'Of course. Can I ask why?'

'I'm not sure,' Daniel answered, still gazing up at the mountain. 'But I've got a feeling I'll soon find out.'

The climb was becoming difficult but Kasheena pressed on. She hadn't made it this far to turn back now. Ascending the mountain was more than just a need. It was a pilgrimage to find the Great Spirit, an expedition into her very soul. She climbed and climbed. When she attained the summit at last, she found a small pool of water and three stones beside it.

It took Daniel three days to reach the mountain and climb to the peak where the old shaman made his home. He was exhausted and badly in need of sleep but he would have to hear what the shaman had to say before he could rest. He saw a campfire burning outside the shaman's lodge and soon he spied the shaman's silhouette among the shadows of the ash trees that grew along the cliffs.

The shaman turned his head. 'You have traveled a long way this night, healer.' He had been standing near the edge of a precipice, gazing into the valley far below.

'Not as far as some have traveled to see you, I'm guessing. I was told that you needed to speak with me about an important matter. Is this true, Great Shaman?'

'No shaman is greater than another. Older and more knowledgeable, perhaps, but certainly not greater. The spirits speak to all people as equals, do they not?'

'I understand. What is it that you wanted to see me about?'

'Healer, there is a village in need of your skills. Desperate need.'

'The village to the north? In the valley below the butte?'

'Yes.' The shaman sounded surprised. 'You've already visited the north village? You're already aware of their needs?'

'No,' Daniel answered. 'I have never been to the north village. No word has reached me that they're in need of my help.'

'Then you've foreseen this?'

'Yes...I mean...I've foreseen that you would send me to the village. I'm pretty sure I know why but there's still a lot that I don't understand.'

The shaman nodded. 'The north village has been without a shaman for a very long time. The spirits of its people have grown weak. Because of this weakness, many have become ill. Some are dying. Your skills as a healer are well known throughout the tribal lands. I have called you to ask you to go to the north village and heal the bodies and spirits of the people.' He paused and Daniel took an involuntary step forward. 'I've called you here to ask you to become shaman of their tribe.'

'I'll go to the village and do what I can to heal the people. I've brought medicines. They're already on the way to the village. I'll do what I can to heal their spirits as well as their bodies, but certainly there are others that are better prepared to become shaman than I am. I love the people of these lands with all my heart, and they've returned that love many times over, but I'm still a foreigner. I was born in a land far away. Many of my ways are still strange to them.' He paused and took a few more steps. 'I've never been the shaman of a tribe before. I'm not sure I'm up to the task.'

'I've already spoken with the elders,' the old shaman assured him. 'It isn't the color of a man's skin or the land where he lives that make him great. It's the things that dwell in his heart and spirit that matter most of all. Healer, the spirits have shown us what is within your heart and spirit. The elders would be honored to have you as their shaman. And so would I.'

Daniel thought long and hard about the shaman's words and the tribe's offer. Joining a tribe as shaman had been his greatest desire for many years but he'd never allowed himself to entertain the idea that one day it might actually happen. Now that this dream was within his grasp, he was hesitant to embrace it.

'What if I fail?' he asked, speaking more to himself than the old shaman. 'Watching over the spirits of an entire tribe is a huge undertaking. A great responsibility. What if I end up doing more harm than good?'

'You do not strike me as a man that fails,' the shaman said. 'At least not at anything you set your heart to.'

A small smile came to Daniel's lips. 'I understand. I'll leave for the north village right away. I'll heal the bodies and spirits of as many as I can. Yes, I will join the tribe as shaman.'

'You have made an old man very happy. I know the elders will be delighted by the news of your decision. But you cannot leave for the village yet. Come and sit with me by the fire, shaman. There's still much we need to discuss.'

Being called shaman touched Daniel. He'd never truly believed that he'd hear the word used in reference to himself. He followed the old shaman to the fire and sat on the ground next to him.

'Before you travel to the north village,' the old man began, 'there's something else I must tell you, something that may be hard for you to understand. I didn't tell you before now because it might have influenced your decision to accept the tribe's offer. That was a decision you had to make on your own.' He turned his head and looked Daniel in the eye. 'The spirits have shown me that there's a member of the north tribe whose life course will be drastically altered by your presence in the village. They have shown me that this person will alter the course of the tribe, and eventually, the future of all the tribes.'

'It's a girl, isn't it?' Daniel asked. It was more a statement than a question. 'A very young girl. She's fiercely brave and as smart as she is reckless.'

'The spirits have shown you this?'

'The spirits? No. I mean, I don't think so. But if I told you, you'd think I'd lost my mind.' Daniel thought about what the old shaman had just told him and how it fitted together with the dream he'd had when he was a boy. If all of this were true, the dream had been a foreshadowing of the future. If it were true, he had dreamed of the girl many years before she had been born. Somehow, he had dreamed of her.

'I don't suppose you know her name, do you?' he asked the old man.

'No.'

'I guess it doesn't matter. Either all of this is really happening or I should be locked up in the nuthouse.'

'What is this house of which you speak? I've never heard of such a house.'

Daniel laughed. 'Now that would be difficult to explain.' He rose to his feet and looked up at the night sky, wondering what oddities the universe would throw his way next. 'I suppose there's only one way to find out what's really happening,' he said. 'I'll just have to go to the north village and see for myself if she's real.'

'You will go to the village soon enough, my friend, but you look very tired. It's many days' journey to the north village, and you won't be of any use if you're bone-weary when you arrive. Stay with me tonight. It's not often that I get company, and there's plenty of room in the lodge for another bed. Stay and sleep. Gather your thoughts and your strength.'

As eager as he was to get to the village, Daniel found the offer too tempting to pass up. He was exhausted. He knew he wouldn't be able to think clearly until he got some rest. 'If it'll make you happy,' he said, 'I will stay here tonight. But if you don't mind, I'd rather sleep out here next to the fire. I have a bedroll to sleep in and I've never spent the night on the top of a mountain. I'd prefer to sleep where I can hear the sounds of the night.'

The old shaman smiled. 'Of course you can sleep next to the fire.

When I was younger, I used to sleep under the stars every chance I got. But now the cold creeps into my bones and makes me stiff and sore. Go ahead. Make up your bed. I have something I need to get from the lodge.' As he pushed himself up and slowly walked to the lodge, Daniel could see that he was in pain. He thought about offering the old man some medication to ease his suffering. 'If he wanted my help he'd ask for it,' he said to himself. He untied his bedroll and laid it on the ground next to the fire.

After several minutes the shaman emerged from the lodge and came back to Daniel. He was holding a staff in his hand. 'This staff was made from an ash tree that grew on this mountain many years before my great-grandfather was born,' he said. He held the staff closer to the fire so Daniel could see it more clearly. 'It was made by the first shaman ever spoken of in the tribal stories. The elders say that he was the first shaman to walk these lands. The shaman that taught me the ways of the spirit medicine gifted it to me more than fifty years ago. Now I gift it to you.'

Daniel was unable to speak. Finally, 'I...I can't accept this from you,' he managed. 'I don't deserve such a gift! I'm honored, of course, but....'

'I will accept no refusal.' The shaman's voice was as hard as stone.

Daniel knew that protesting wasn't going to change anything and that to resist further would be to risk offending him and dishonoring the spirit in which the staff was being offered. He would have to accept the shaman's gift. 'I don't know what to say. Thank you doesn't come close to covering it.'

The old man's eyes twinkled. 'Just use it wisely and think about the old man that gave it to you from time to time.' He placed the staff in Daniel's hand and patted him on the shoulder. 'That will be thanks enough.' He pointed at the bedroll. 'Young shaman, you should sleep now. The days ahead will be eventful.'

Daniel laid the staff across his duffle bag and crawled into his bedroll. Lying next to the fire felt wonderful and even though his *mind was full of thoughts, he began to drift toward sleep. The old shaman walked to the other side of the fire and sat on the ground before it to get warm. Daniel could no longer resist the urge to sleep, and just before he closed his eyes, he saw a dragonfly buzz past his head and come to rest on the shaman's shoulder. He began to dream....*

Kasheena's heart raced as she neared the pool. She would see the face of the Great Spirit in its surface. At last she would know what the Great Spirit truly was. She knelt before the pool and slowly leaned forward. Nothing. Not even her own reflection. 'What's wrong?' *she asked herself.* 'Maybe I wasn't ready, after all.' *She sat back on her heels.* 'Maybe the ancestors were wrong. Maybe the dream was just a dream, not an omen for me to climb the mountain.'

A light rain began to fall and the raindrops sent ripples flowing over the surface of the pool. Kasheena leaned forward again. Was she seeing something among the ripples? It looked like a face. With newfound hope, she bent closer to the pool and concentrated her vision. Another ripple flowed over the pool's surface. This time she was sure she saw something. ' The Great Spirit is a turtle?'

Another ripple. Now she saw the face of her grandmother. Another ripple. She saw a baby being born. Another. She saw an old man crying in pain. The rain began to fall harder and soon the surface of the pool was fully disturbed. Within each ripple, Kasheena could see a different image. She could feel *them. But, she suddenly realized, they weren't images. She was seeing visions. Visions of everything she had ever seen and everyone she had ever known.*

And there were other visions. Many of the things she was seeing she didn't recognize. Visions of unfamiliar people and places that were somehow connected to all the others. Connected, she thought. Realization was dawning in her. The Great Spirit was close. Suddenly she heard the old woman's voice in her mind: ' If you look hard enough, you will see me many times in many things. Seek me in your spirit, Child. Seek me in your heart.'

She had learned the final lesson.

The rain slowed and the ripples diminished. She was no longer seeing the things she needed to see. Now she was seeing what she wanted to see. She saw the faces of her mother and father. She saw the faces of her tribe. She saw the birdman and the old woman. She saw Daniel. The rain stopped and the pool became still. Gazing upon its surface, Kasheena finally saw the face of the Great Spirit. It was her own reflection.

The Great Spirit wasn't something mysterious and unknowable. It wasn't one thing. It was all things. Even she was a part of it.

Suddenly Kasheena felt very sleepy. She felt herself drifting away, and she soon realized that she was no longer on the mountaintop gazing down at her reflection in the pool. Now she was on the other side of the reflection gazing up at herself. She began to drift further away, floating down toward sleep. Toward her next destination. She could no longer keep her eyes open and just before she closed them, she thought she saw The Three sitting on the stones that surrounded the pool. They were looking down at her, and for the first time Kasheena could see the shaman's face. She began to dream....

Sacred Sparks

One thing about trains. It doesn't matter where they're going. What matters is deciding to get on. - *The Polar Express* The Movie

You will now undertake the fourth and final leg of your spiritual journey. This will be a pilgrimage back through the ages and you will attempt to witness the first sacred spark of human spirituality. As I explained earlier in this book, my theory on this subject is highly speculative and thus highly subject to interpretation. What the *sacred spark* means to me might mean something entirely different to you. All I'm offering you is a glimpse into one possible past.

To refresh your memory, it is my contention that at some

point in humanity's past, there was a tribe that predated the beginnings of recorded history by millennia, and perhaps some member of that ancient tribe realized for the very first time that there was something more than just 'us.' Something larger than the human self, something even larger than the tribe. This something, I believe, was (and still is) an invisible essence that connects everyone and everything in the universe together: It is this essential being, this 'sacred spark' of something, that crept into our human imagination to give humankind the ability to leap beyond logic and perceive more than we can touch with our hands and see with our eyes. I believe that it was this spark of imagination and perception of the unseen that eventually led to the development of human spirituality and religion.

At what point in the past humans first became aware of unseen forces is unknown. New fossil evidence suggests that the first *Homo sapiens* roamed Africa around 195,000 years ago, but awareness of incorporeal beings and forces probably came much later. For example, the cave paintings at Chauvet (the earliest known) were made around 32,000 years ago, and the famous Venus of Willendorf statue is estimated to have been carved between 22,000 and 24,000 years ago.

All we know for certain is that at some point in the past, human awareness of the unseen *did* begin. The goal of this final leg of your journey, therefore, is to rejoin the Great Tribe and, by way of shamanic traveling, follow the tribe back through time and attempt to experience what it might have been like to be the first person to become aware of the unseen. Because this journey is subjective and thus open to personal interpretation, I will give you a set of instructions, followed by visualizations of things you *might* see and experience on your journey; these are not necessarily things you *will* see and experience. You should consider the visualizations I create as possibilities rather than absolutes. Consider them mental stimulants to get your spiritual juices flowing in the right direction.

If you are ready, allow me to lead you into the spirit lands and back through time. Let us search for the origin of human spirituality and gain insight into our own spiritual needs.

Shamanic Traveling Path Four:

The Pilgrimage

The preparation and technique for your fourth adventure in shamanic traveling will be the same as on your previous travels. If you've skipped over any of the work in this book, you should go back and complete it before undertaking this final leg of your journey. If the goal of the journey is in any way unclear, spend some time re-reading the previous chapter and meditating on the goal before you proceed. For ease of use, I will separate the instructions from the visualizations. The instructions will appear in plain text. The visualizations will directly follow the instructions in italics.

As always, you will begin the final leg of your journey by entering into the spirit lands. *Enter into the spirit lands, and slowly make your way to the base camp. Take your time and don't rush. Closely observe any inhabitants of the spirit lands you encounter along the way. Make note of anything that looks or feels different than it did on your previous travels.*

As you enter the spirit lands, everything is silent and calm. It almost seems as though the land itself is aware of the sacredness of your journey and has been patiently awaiting your arrival. The inhabitants of the spirit lands look upon you knowingly. You can feel their life force and the energy of the spirit lands all around you.

As you near the base camp, you see that you have a visitor who has come to speak with you of your journey. You spend some time talking with this person and you become impassioned by the conversation. The goal of your journey is now clearer and more meaningful than ever before. You are eager to continue your pilgrimage.

Once you've arrived at the base camp, proceed through the gateway of the first medicine wheel and enter into the lower world.

As you enter the gateway of the first medicine wheel, you feel its power and energy flowing all around you. The energy makes you feel strong and determined. Your spirit feels mystical and free. The energies of the medicine wheel envelop you and you feel yourself slowly being pulled downward toward the lower world.

When you have arrived in the lower world, use the skills you have learned to make contact with the wolf spirit and ask it for advice. Bask in the energy of the wolf spirit until you own spirit feels wild and free. Thank the wolf spirit for its counsel and proceed to the inner medicine wheel.

As you enter the lower world, you are exhilarated by its primal power. The animal spirits of the lower world gather all around you as though to give credence and meaning to your journey. Among these spirits there is one whose spiritual force you can feel above the others. This is the wolf and it has come to give counsel and lend you its wild energy. He is so close you can see into his eyes and feel his warm breath on your skin. The wolf shows you visions of the things he wants you to know. You can see these visions clearly in your mind. You bask in the wildness of his spiritual energy. You feel your own spirit growing wild and free. When the wolf tells you that it is time to continue your journey, you thank it for its counsel and energy. You continue through the lower world toward the inner medicine wheel.

At the inner medicine wheel, clearly state your purpose and intent, either aloud or in your mind. Walk along the wheel's perimeter, feeling its energy as you go. Walk the edge of the wheel until you have located the spoke that leads to the tribal land. Visualize the Great Tribe in your mind. Build the vision until the spoke of the medicine wheel begins to change and becomes a pathway before you. Walk the pathway and enter into the tribal land.

As you approach the inner wheel, your anticipation grows stronger. You are excited about returning to the land of the Great Tribe. You speak your intention to join the tribe on their sacred pilgrimage. You slowly walk the perimeter of the medicine wheel, feeling the energies of the spokes as you walk. When you locate the spoke that leads to the tribal land, you visualize the Great Tribe in your mind. You envision the tribe until you can see the faces of the people and even hear their voices. You build this vision until you can feel the presence of the Great Tribe all around you. The spoke of the wheel begins to change. It becomes a pathway to the tribal land, and soon the pathway opens up before you. As you step on the pathway, you can hear the voices of the tribe calling for you to join them. You follow along the pathway until it leads you the tribal land.

Once you have reached the tribal land and rejoined the Great Tribe, you will set off with them on a long journey. This journey is a pilgrimage to the motherland of the Great Tribe's ancestors. You are venturing to the native land of the first human tribe. As you travel to this native land, you will be traveling back through time. You will travel back in time until you arrive at the age of the first human tribe. You will then move forward through time until you come upon the first sacred spark of human spirituality. You will witness the birth of this spark. Once this goal has been accomplished, you will return to the lower world and ascend to the spirit lands. Finally you will return to your shamanic room and re-enter the waking world of consensual reality.

The tribal land is as silent as the spirit lands were but here you see much more activity. The Great Tribe is quietly preparing for a long journey. They appear serene and blissful in their work. There is an unspoken understanding between you and members of the tribe and you join them as they set off. You are journeying to the land of the first ancestors. In the blink of an eye you have traveled a thousand miles away from the tribal land and a thousand years back through time. Now you are trekking across a great plain. You can see snow-capped mountain peaks looming in the distance.

Another blink, and now you are traveling with the Great Tribe across a great bridge of ice that joins two continents. You have now traveled 30,000 years back through time. As you watch, the tribe slowly begins to change. You begin to change as well. Outward signs and symbols of the tribe's spiritual beliefs are becoming more archaic. Some have disappeared altogether. Everything around you feels primal and ancient. You feel primal and ancient.

Another blink and you are traveling with the tribe across a desert that stretches for as far as the eye can see. You have traveled 100,000 years back through time, and almost nothing remains of the spiritual beliefs the Great Tribe once held. They wear no jewelry or face paint. They carry no drums or staffs. You see that one of the tribal elders carries a small, crudely carved statue of a divine being in her hand. Other than the statue, nothing remains of the tribe's once great spiritual beliefs.

Another blink and you are walking with the tribe through an immense jungle. You have now traveled nearly 200,000 years back through time. You have arrived in the motherland of the first human tribe. You see the shadowy figure of someone standing just ahead of you in the jungle, and as you near this person, you know that you are gazing upon the face of the first true human. You behold the Great Mother. She is the source of modern hominid life, the matriarch of all humankind. When you look deep within her eyes, you see a hazy vision of one of her descendants.

Now you begin to move slowly forward in time, and as you do, the vision of the descendant you glimpsed becomes clearer and clearer, until at last you find yourself standing next to the descendant, high atop a hill that overlooks a gently sloping valley. You gaze into the valley far below, and you suddenly realize that you are no longer looking through your own eyes. You are now seeing the world through the eyes of the descendant of the Great Mother. The descendant is aware only of the world around her. She knows nothing beyond what she has seen with her own eyes and touched with her own hands. She knows nothing of spirituality or religion. Pitch-black storm clouds are forming in the skies over the valley. You have become one with the descendant. You can no longer *imagine anything beyond the storm clouds you see. You can imagine nothing beyond the storm. You only know that soon it will begin to rain.*

Suddenly, a brilliant flash of lightning illuminates the sky, a tremendous crash of thunder rolls through the valley. You look into the storm above you, and, just for a moment, you see a familiar shape take form in one of the clouds: it seems to be the shape of a human face. Something begins to stir and awaken within you. It is a dawning awareness unlike anything you have ever known.

Another flash lights up the sky and your awareness increases. It grows until, at last, understanding blossoms in your mind. A cold chill washes over your body as you realize for the very first time that something exists beyond what you can see and touch. You are filled with wonderment as you realize that forces exist beyond what your senses are capable of perceiving. For the very first time, you are aware of a force that is larger than yourself, larger than the tribe.

Suddenly, you are seeing the world through your own eyes again. You turn your head and look upon the descendant of the Great Mother. She is your ancestor! She is the first ancestor to become aware of the unseen. Slowly, everything around you begins to change. You are moving forward through time. The ancestor now wears a beaded necklace and has symbols painted on her face. You move forward though time again. Now the ancestor carries a staff adorned with feathers. You watch as she paints pictures on cave walls. You move further and further forward through time, and suddenly you are back in the tribal land with the Great Tribe. Your ancestor is numbered among them. She gives you a knowing look.

You feel your mind and spirit floating away from the tribe and you soon find yourself walking along the path that leads to the lower world. You enter the lower world and look down at the medicine wheel and imagine where the other spokes might lead. You ascend to the spirit land, and far off in the distance you see a soft glow of light. As you walk toward this light, you look all around. You can feel the Great Spirit dwelling within everything you see. The glowing light becomes brighter and brighter, until it is all you can see with your eyes and in your mind.

You open your eyes and return to the waking world. The fire of the Great Spirit burns in your heart.

Now that you have completed the final leg of the journey, spend some time contemplating what you have seen and experienced. I hope you have enjoyed the adventure as much as I have,and I thank you for allowing me to walk with you for a time down your spiritual path. At long last, our journey together has nearly come to an end. The spirit lands and medicine wheels are at your disposal for as long as you care to use them. Many more adventures beyond my imagining await you. You have tended the embers and built the fire of the Great Spirit within. All that's left to do is claim the third and final medicine wheel. This is the *sun wheel*.

Emergence Part Five:

In Dreams Awake

Kasheena awoke at the top of a steep hill a few miles from her village. By the blackness of the sky and the brilliance of the stars overhead, she could tell it must be the middle of the night. She'd just had the strangest dream. The memory of it was still fresh in her mind. Sitting up, she wiped the sleep from her eyes and looked around. She couldn't remember how she'd gotten to the top of the hill, or even what she was doing up here. All at once she spied the silhouette of the old shaman. He was sitting next to a small campfire near the edge of the overlook. Now she remembered. She had fallen very ill and he had brought her to the top of the hill to heal her. The hilltop was the shaman's favorite place to practice his medicine. He'd once told her that the spirits were strong here, that their presence helped to heal the sick. Smiling, Kasheena rose to her feet and walked over to him. She saw that he was wrapped in a blanket, gazing up at the stars.

'Grandfather...' she said as she sat on the ground next to him and placed her arm around his shoulders, 'Daniel. I've just had the strangest dream! It seemed to go on forever. In my dream I traveled to many places and met extraordinary people.'

'Tell me more about your dream,' the shaman said.

'Well,' she began, 'It's kind of hard to explain but I think the dream was mostly about my parents and all the things you've taught me over the years. I've never told you about my parents, have I? Have I ever told you how they died?'

'No,' he replied. 'I know your memories of them are painful, so I never asked you to talk about them.'

'My father was a great warrior who dedicated his life to protecting the village. He was a big, powerful man but he was wise and had a kind heart. If he hadn't died, he would have become chieftain. My mother was a wise woman. She knew how to use herbs and plants to cure illness. She was the village storyteller too and she kept scrolls of tribal lore that were passed down to her by the elders. They were killed during an attack by a tribe of outlanders.' She sighed a deep sigh. 'I've always blamed my father for my mother's death. I never forgave him for not being able to protect her.'

After a pause the shaman nodded. 'The elders have told me about the outlanders and their attack on the village,' he said in a soft voice. 'They told me that at the time of the attack, many of the tribe's warriors were away on a hunting party. They also told me that if it hadn't been for your father's strength and bravery, the village would have been overrun. They said he fought back many warriors before he fell. His courage saved many lives.'

A tear came to Kasheena's eye. 'My mother wouldn't leave him. When the attack came, he told her to take me to safety, but she refused. She sent my grandmother and me into the forest to hide. She fought at his side. She died for no reason.'

'She died doing what she thought was right.'

'I think I understand that now.' She wiped her eyes. 'I no longer blame him for her death. You know, they were with me in my dream. They didn't look at all like I remember, though. Their faces kept changing. But I'm certain it was them. I dreamed of you, too. I dreamed about all the lessons you've given me. I dreamed about all the life lessons I've learned.'

'Dreams are peculiar things,' the shaman began. 'Some people believe that dreams are nothing more than the flights of our imaginations. Some believe that they are visions given to us by the Great Spirit.'

'Daniel, what do you believe?'

The shaman looked at her and smiled. His face was old and wrinkled, worn by time and the sun but pleasing to look upon all the same. 'I believe it doesn't matter what dreams are or where they come from. I believe dreams are a part of life. I believe it's good to be alive.'

Kasheena snuggled closer to her old friend, and they sat still for a time, gazing into the night sky together.

'I'm feeling much better,' she told him when the moon was near dawn's horizon. 'Will we be going back to the village soon?'

'In the morning,' he said. 'At dawn, you will return to the village and speak with the elders. They will have much to discuss with you. I will not be going.'

'What do you mean you won't be going? If you have other things to do, I can come along and help.'

The old shaman peered into the dark and breathed deeply of the night air. 'Where I'm going you cannot follow,' he said. 'At least not yet. Tonight I will fly with the spirits to the Great Ancestors. I will join them in the next world and take my place at their side.'

'No!' she whispered, her lips trembling. 'No! You can't leave me... not yet. Stay with me a while longer. Stay and teach me'

'I've already taught you everything I know.' He smiled at her again. 'And you've become a far greater shaman than I could have hoped you'd be. Girl, your strength and bravery are unmatched. You're wise beyond your years. I've watched you grow from a reckless girl into an extraordinary young woman. Now it's your turn to watch over the spirits of your people. It's time for you to take your rightful place as shaman of the tribe.'

'But there's never been a female shaman before. What if the tribe won't accept me? What if I'm not ready? What if I fail?'

Daniel laughed and then started coughing. 'Someone I knew a very long time ago spoke those exact same words,' he managed to say through the coughing. 'Despite his own insecurity, he became a fine shaman. He healed the spirits of many people.'

'Who was he, Grandfather?'

'Me.'

Daniel coughed again, and his hands began to tremble. He was very tired and he knew that he would need to sleep very soon. 'I've already spoken with the elders,' he said, his voice raspy now. 'They know I won't be returning to the village. I've told them. You are to become shaman in my place. This is your destiny.' He reached behind him and picked up his staff. 'You must embrace your destiny if the tribes are to survive. The staff is yours now. It's very old, you know. It was made by the first shaman ever to walk these lands.' He laid the staff across Kasheena's knees. 'When you carry it, think of me from time to time'

Kasheena wrapped her arms around her old friend. The screech of a hawk sounded somewhere in the distance and Daniel looked longingly into the night sky. He relaxed his posture, laid his head on her shoulder and closed his eyes for the last time.

Kasheena sat in silence, listening to the sounds of the night. The shadows of the windswept pines washed over her, making her look much older than she really was. Daniel was with the Great Ancestors now. Now she could only visit him in dreams. Now she would only hear his voice in the wind. She sat with him through the night, remembering what he had taught her.

And at dawn, she stood up and laid the old man carefully on his side. She fashioned a travois from two fallen tree branches and Daniel's hide coat, then wrapped his body in the makeshift stretcher. Gathering her own belongings, including the turtle shell and healing stone that had once belonged to her mother and stowing them in her leather sack, she took the staff in hand and began a long and slow descent to the village. Daniel would have wanted her to leave his body at the top of the hill. It's only an empty husk he would have told her, but she knew the tribe would want to see him one last time.

By the time she reached the village, it was well past sunset. The chieftain and the elders were gathered around the central fire in anticipation of her return. A young warrior who fancied her was waiting as well, and upon seeing her, he ran to her side and helped pull the travois to the fireside.

Kasheena sat with the elders for many hours, discussing her future with the tribe. Come the next dawn, she was to be ordained as shaman, and there would be a small ceremony to honor her *accession. Once the elders had spoken their piece, she walked silently beside the young warrior to her lodge. She thanked him for his help and gave him a kiss on the cheek, then went inside. She set her leather sack on the floor at the foot of her bed and the staff in a corner of the room. Running her fingers over the hawk feathers tied to its shaft, she thought of Daniel again. The hawk had been a symbol of his medicine for as long as she could remember.*

Knowing she had to get some sleep, she crawled into bed, but she lay awake for a time, thinking of the days to come. Her first acts as shaman would be to oversee Daniel's burial rite and ease the spirits of her people. Finally she began to drift into sleep. Her last thought was the single word Daniel had spoken before he had passed into the next world.

Dreamwalker.

A dragonfly flew through an open window and came to rest on her pillow. She began to dream…

Tending the Fires Goal Four:

The Sun Wheel

The sun wheel is the third medicine wheel I described to you earlier in this book. You may recall that the spokes of the third wheel radiate out, rather than in. If you don't remember what the third wheel looks like, refer to the diagram on page (X). The sun wheel differs from the other medicine wheels in that it isn't a wheel you will find in the spirit lands or the lower world, but a wheel that you yourself are a part of. I am also a part of the sun wheel, as are all those who seek the spiritual light within themselves.

Many years ago, before I knew anything of metaphysical or spiritual practice, night after night I was compelled to get out of bed and I would sit on the floor in my living room before a lit candle asking myself a single question: *What do you want from me?* Some unseen force was trying to get my attention. Something was calling out to me, but at that time I didn't know what it was. I was just one little light sitting in the darkness searching for meaning. Thinking back on it now, I realize that as far as I have traveled on my spiritual journey, I am still just one little light in the darkness searching for meaning. There are many dark places in our world, and at times it seems that there are too few lights to illuminate them. But when I close my eyes and picture that candle in my mind, now I see other little lights, and I know that I am not alone.

We are not alone. We are collectively a spiritual being with a radiant spirit. We are each an integral part of the sun wheel. As each of our lights combines with the next, for one small moment in time we are all connected. For one small moment we are as one. We are shamans. We are *tribe....*

Emergence Part Six:

No Stories End

Kasheena awoke in her bed under the lean-to she lived in with her grandmother. Any other day she would have lain under the covers for a time, warm and cozy and wondering at her dreams. Not today. Today was a special day. There would be no time for lying around or playing with the other children. The tribe was welcoming a new shaman, a man said to have come from a far away land. He was a handsome man with pale skin and a funny name. The shaman, who had arrived a few days before, had told Kasheena that he had dreamed of her when he was a little boy. Somehow, he said, he had dreamed of her many years before she had been born. She had overheard the shaman tell the elders that after sunset he would travel to the top of the hill and speak with the spirits. Kasheena planned to spend the day doing her chores and gathering firewood for her grandmother. Tonight, though, she would follow the shaman in secret in hopes of catching even a small glimpse of his medicine.

Footnotes

1 Areas of study that deal with the study of human society and the individual relationships with society. This may include study areas such as psychology, sociology, anthropology, and political science.

2 A now common name that was first applied to a large stone structure in Northern Wyoming known as the Big Horn Medicine Wheel.

3 Information compiled from materials supplied by the Provincial Museum of Alberta, Canada.

4 I was unable to locate any information as to a specific person who first used this term, only that it was applied to the Big Horn Medicine Wheel by 'white men' near the end of the 19th century.

5 More information can be found at http://www.pma.edmonton.ab.ca/human/archaeo/faq/med whls.htm

6 Hillary S. Webb, *Exploring Shamanism*, (New Jersey: Career Press/New Page Books, 2003). 77

7 Mircea Eliade, *Shamanism, Archaic Techniques of Ecstasy* (Princeton, NJ: Princeton University Press, 1964, 1992), 174-175.

8 Jack Tresidder, *The Complete Dictionary of Symbols* (San Francisco, Ca: Chronicle Books LLC, 2005) 158

9 Jack Tresidder, *The Complete Dictionary of Symbols* (San Francisco: Chronicle Books, 2005).

10 The widely used and commonly recognized symbol of modern Witchcraft and neopaganism.

11 Agni is the Hindu fire god who is said to have consumed his parents upon his birth because of their inability to provide for him. This is symbolic of the fire, which is created by rubbing two sticks together. The fire consumes

its 'parental' sticks.

12 Clarissa Pinkóla Estés *Women Who Run With the Wolves, Myths and Stories of the Wild Woman Archetype-* (New York. Ballantine Books, 1992)

13 *Personal communication. Carol Rozinski, Michigan*

Bibliography

Eliade, Mircea. *Shamanism, Archaic Techniques of Ecstasy* (Princeton, NJ: Princeton University Press, 1964, 1992), 174-175.

Estés, Clarissa Pinkola. *Women Who Run With the Wolves, Myths and Stories of the Wild Woman Archetype-* (New York. Ballantine Books, 1992).

Tresidder, Jack. *The Complete Dictionary of Symbols* (San Francisco, Ca: Chronicle Books LLC, 2005) 158.

Webb, Hillary S. *Exploring Shamanism*, (New Jersey: Career Press/New Page Books, 2003), 77.

Author Name: Marcus F. Griffin

Legal Name: Marc William Brower   Address: 1239 Canton St Elkhart, IN 46514

Phone: 574-612-3000

Email: Marcusfgriffin@comcast.net

BOOKS

O is a symbol of the world, of oneness and unity. In different cultures it also means the "eye," symbolizing knowledge and insight. We aim to publish books that are accessible, constructive and that challenge accepted opinion, both that of academia and the "moral majority."

Our books are available in all good English language bookstores worldwide. If you don't see the book on the shelves ask the bookstore to order it for you, quoting the ISBN number and title. Alternatively you can order online (all major online retail sites carry our titles) or contact the distributor in the relevant country, listed on the copyright page.

See our website www.o-books.net for a full list of over 500 titles, growing by 100 a year.

And tune in to myspiritradio.com for our book review radio show, hosted by June-Elleni Laine, where you can listen to the authors discussing their books.